THE TRUMP ERA

A BOOK OF POETRY

GERALD W. KING

Dorrance Publishing Co
585 Alpha Drive
Pittsburgh, PA 15238
Visit our website at www.dorrancebookstore.com

ISBN: 979-8-8860-4040-1
eISBN: 979-8-8860-4943-5

In loving memory of
Erma L. King and Kathrine M. Turner

TRUMP'S EVIL WILL NOT PREVAIL!

Racist actions and violence are not what our country is about;

Trump with his friends and supporters would like to change all
    that, there's no doubt.

The idiot conspirators who helped put his Capitol riot mob to-
    gether

Thought what they did was really something very clever/

However, guys, you didn't get away with it. Not so fast!

The investigative authorities are focused on it, and however
    long it takes, it will last.

They are definitely working hard on their leads to find out;

It will be known A.S.A.P., without a doubt,

Those being exposed and charged are coming, and not far away;

Eventually, the ones responsible are going to have their day.

It won't take forever; remember, never say never,

Because this is so serious, authorities won't say, "oh…whatever…"

Trump's looking at numerous cases of legal litigation;

No one else has ever faced as many throughout our nation.

He's definitely the leader in all those legal things;

It's not something a good person wants to be connected with,
    and all the negativity it brings.

When Trump was running for president, Republicans were say-
    ing his candidacy would be grand;

Turns out, all they were doing was pulling a really big scam!

Good life is about righteousness, being fair to one another;
that's what it's all about.

We've been experiencing the opposite—that's clearly no doubt.

Trump's mind set is; he doesn't believe goodness exists.

We've got to fight against that mentality and have to constantly
persist.

There are two major problems we're facing: coronavirus and
bad politics.

The only way to fix it is right answers and no nasty, dirty tricks.

In these days and times, one political party is clearly being untrue;

We've got to work hard to overturn that problem for everybody
and not just a few.

We have to fight real hard; the soul of America is at stake.

It has to be done immediately—if not, we're headed for a really
bad fate.

Trump only wants to make big money for himself all the time,
day and night.

Take that ability away from him, he'll stop and won't continue
to put up a fight.

MORE OF TRUMP'S AWFUL MESS!

In the 2020 election when President Trump was defeated,
He spoke out stating a fraudulent LIE, saying he had been
  cheated;
The same time that happened, he asked a state official to find
  him thousands of votes—
That shows he's the real cheater, and that's really no joke!
It also shows he's actually the one who openly finds ways to cheat,
Always being obvious and not ever being discreet.
He always uses the same old lying tactics and themes,
And he also manages to come up with new lying ways and
  schemes,
Does anybody think he'll eventually change, or could he ever stop?
I've got to say, honestly, I really think not.
That's also like thinking a wild leopard would change his spots.
Trump makes dirty money, hand over foot, all the time;
There's a need to investigate his actions for any illegal crimes,
There are a lot of people who enable him, making him even
  worse;
The list of names goes on and on…I can't think who's really first.
Donald Trump without a doubt runs the Republican Party,
And their main theme and goal is to be the country's ultimate
  authority.
Trump and honesty—those terms have never really matched.

B.S., fake news, and deception are the only things combined
    and are definitely attached.
Fake news and bamboozling his followers; makes them think
    he's their master;
His dirty moves and shenanigans have pushed the country to-
    wards disaster.

With all the chaos and misdeeds, those things he hopes will blend,
We've got to put our minds together to bring all this mess to an
    end.
The January 6 committee have a lot against the ex-president;
What they've announced to the public concludes the negativity
    is very much quite evident.

TRUMP NEGATIVITY
SEEMS TO NEVER END!

The U.S. Department of Justice recently spoke up, and what
was told?

How Trump had been proven hateful and also very bold.

On January 6, 2021, he shouted out a bunch of rhetoric and
evil nasty lies

To get his raunchy M.A.G.A crowd pumped up and emo-
tionally radicalized.

We're being tested negatively at the government's highest level

By a mindset that's not far from being comparable to the devil.

It's coming from those politicians who won't do things consid-
ered right,

Splitting the masses down the middle, divided for an ugly fight.

Under any known circumstances, it's not a justified position;

Looking at it from any logical viewpoint, or under any logical
conditions,

This is what happens when you mentally weaponize an ugly
crowd:

They'll do dirty, nasty, evil things up front and say it clearly
out loud.

Is there something wrong with Trump? You think maybe it's
water on the brain?

He doesn't seem to think clearly or logically as though he's not
  completely sane,
It's unusual how Trump manages to control some politicians;
They've lost their sense of keeping the country safe under all pa-
  triotic conditions.
Their sense of country first is clearly and completely off track,
Along with being completely unhinged and definitely out of
  whack.
Looking at all the evidence, you'll see it's definitely a fact.

Anyone with common sense knows that it's all true;
It's been that way for quite a while and is really nothing new.
Everything ever written about Trump is the same and very clear:
He completely failed as the president for all four years.

I'M LOST FOR WORDS ABOUT TRUMP!

When Trump left the White House, we thought his control was done.

However, the nightmare wasn't over; it had only just begun.

Bad politics now at the state level seems to be widespread;

Trumpism everywhere is alive and well, and not completely dead.

We need all good leaders to step up and meet this crisis head on;

If they don't do this immediately, democracy could very well be gone.

What kind of society will be there for our children? What will be left for them?

Do we explain it's the new normal way of living and a normal trend?

However, we must say it's a challenge and a fight that will definitely NOT end;

This country started with a fight, and now it continues, and that's how it will always be

In order to keep our society open to all people and always be free.

Trump's working towards another term as president in 2024;

There are a lot of people working to make sure to never unlock that door!

There are also great hopes the decisions made during that general election

Send a clear message and a final decision of total rejection.

Our country surely cannot ever endure anymore;

Four more years of Trump madness, for sure.

Trump's record indicates he's actually a criminal; that's big time.

If he ever gets to be president again, look for even bigger crimes.

Let's stop the Trump madness, immediately; right now;

By stopping his re-election bid, that is simply how.

Stopping him from getting back in the White House will be
doing a crucial job,

And that kind of message will probably silence his angry, ugly
mob.

Our diverse country of voters at the next general election needs
to step up and right in,

Pull everything together for a major, decisive win.

We have to show Trump we're not stupid and not blind and can
see all the evil, ugly signs

Of his intentions being not good and showing us what's on his
evil, crooked mind.

TRUMP WANTED TO BE EMPEROR!

Trump's clown show, we all do know will definitely go…

Not up to heaven, but way down below.

That's not a good place where decent people want to go to;

That's Trump's peoples place easily said, with really quite a view.

He lies all the time and doesn't really mind giving his kids that mentality and vision,

Then cheated other family members, not caring about their feelings and negative divisions.

His family business was ordered to stop all its operations

Due to the illegal activities in New York when determined were state violations.

That kind of evilness will never rest; completely opposite of the best.

His power with Republicans for some reason always keeps going on,

Even though his power in the world is no longer strong,

How dumb can his supporters be with the clear evidence and facts?

Even though everybody else can see all his ignorant and stupid crap,

By a wing and a prayer, he wants to hold on to his former office and place,

But all he can really hold on to is his total historical disgrace,

Mark my word; he's going to try his best to get it all back.

We've got to be vigilant, strong, and make sure to stop his cam-
paign attacks.

The courts all ruled, his financial documents were inaccurate,
overblown and completely outrageous.

Those same actions, he taught to his kids—it's like it's contagious.

He goes on and on with B.S. that seems to never fail;

The only way to stop his madness is put him under the jail.

GOD help us, please! We need Your help to stop his evil plans
to steal

The presidency back and be the boss. That's the way a lot of
people feel.

It was a dark day in America when he was elected the top boss.

It's now over four years later, and we're still paying a horrible
cost.

FINALLY

We must make it clearly known for all times:

Bottom line, Donald Trump will never, ever shine.

Whatever evilness he's ever done...

JUSTICE for however long it takes...will eventually come!

TRUMP FACING POSSIBLE BAD CHARGES!

To date, Trump's horrible actions are no surprise and widely in
the know;
All the information on what he's done is ongoing and still has
room to grow.
This is an issue Donald Trump definitely doesn't want us to see:
Congressional investigations have increased proceedings to get
all the information they need.
All this research is very important for the truth, we do agree;
All of Trump's people who've always been on the frontline and
stalking,
They've all clammed up quickly and are no longer talking.
Things are closing in on him right now, and he's really in a vice.
That's not a comfortable position to be in; it doesn't feel very nice.
Time is closing in real soon for Trump to pay all his dues.
There's no one he's focused on right now that he thinks he can sue.
"He who laughs last laughs loudest" is a saying from past
times—
We can now laugh at Donald Trump; he'll be paying for all his
crimes.
Right now, I wouldn't want to be in Donald Trump's shoes;
There's so much bad stuff he's facing; he's not sure who is who.
The flood gates have opened up, and the dam has finally
broken;

Everyone who's against him is speaking out, and some have already spoken,

Anybody who knows something important, it's time to step up to the plate.

Things are about to get really heated up, even worse than Watergate!

Trump's probably now saying, "Everybody, please give me a break."

Sorry. That's not going to happen. There's no time to waste and too much at stake.

Trump's daughter Ivanka was summoned to speak up and spill the unknown beans.

If she knows what's in her best interest, she better come completely clean.

When Don Junior's turn comes up to speak, he'd better do the same,

Because if he doesn't come clean, he'll find out, they aren't playing games.

DONALD TRUMP: A DERELICT PRESIDENT!

From 2016 to 2020, Donald Trump was a derelict president,

Convicted twice while he was in office and the residing White
House resident,

Congress documented everything available that they knew and
saw,

Everything presented showed them; he was breaking a number
of laws.

The time when he was the executive branch leader and ob-
viously the boss,

Many things he did and were done at that time put the country
at a great loss.

At that time, the United Sates was at a point of serious reckoning,

All because of his lies, misinformation, chaos, and heckling.

In the history of our country, there's never been a person who'd
put us in that position.

What he did while in office proved to us, he's really not a politician;

Just a non-intelligent, fake conman on a major power grab mission.

Arrogant, coldblooded, and non-compassionate describes
Trump's personality as a man;

Totally power-hungry, seeking enormous power control was his
master plan.

As president for four years, his decisions for the country were
something no one could understand,

No different than when he was a businessman, always looking
  for loyal fans.
If that type of person ever became our president again, our de-
  mocracy wouldn't survive;
The United Stated of America as we know it, would roll over
  and die.

Because of this major issue, we must stay focused and continue
  to fight
To keep our country safe and moving forward and forever
  doing what's right.
Trump's focus is making more money for himself; that's his ulti-
  mate goal.
That's part of the reason he keeps spreading lies about the elec-
  tion he says the Democrats stole.
All his political appointees' performances proved to be a hor-
  rible disgrace,
Knocking our country's normal traditions and ideologies way
  off base;
Trump continues to keep motivating his M.A.G.A. people with
  his evil and nasty charm,
Relentlessly continuing to create and putting our country in po-
  sition to face great harm.
He's still working hard to change the rules against all citizens'
  right to vote...
We can't tolerate that mess anymore; we should treat this as a
  stupid Trump joke,

What's the next evil, nasty irregularity he will throw directly at us?
We'll probably discuss our mistrust when he says something
    that's disgusting.
What he also does is say anything dumb that comes to his mind;
Whatever he says, it's usually not good—we'll definitely find
    out in due time!

TRUMP: HIS DOWNFALLS
ARE OFF THE MAP!

There's quite a large list of Trump's misdeeds, in which he was
    deeply involved;

Some are definitely known to us, and most are still unsolved.

A number of the misdeeds are tied up in litigations;

People everywhere are upset about all those still pending situations.

They feel he shouldn't be treated with any extra special care—

Not treated better than anyone else; just wouldn't be seen as fair.

All we're asking for now is the legal system to work faster

To stop Trump from being able to create another phony or fake
    disaster.

This is what he's the master at:

Always starting up more crap,

And we surely don't need that.

There were numerous political sympathizers who helped the in-
    surrection go on;

We've got to weed them out completely, ensuring our focus
    stays strong.

And if we do everything needed, forever they'll be gone.

We need to strengthen our actions more than just vote every
    two to four years.

If we toe the mark and work hard, we can eliminate our fears.

Time's moved on, and we're now in the year 2022;

Trump and his supporters are now saying they're not com-
    pletely through.
It's sad to see all their chaos still continuing on
With them having no evidence or proof means; it's the same old
    stupid song.
Seemingly though, this entire rhetoric is quite our vicious curse;
We've got to figure out a way to put all this in reverse.
The Department of Justice is working very hard every single day
To make sure all this criminality is behind us completely and
    forever gone away.
Our country, for over the past 220-plus years,
Has been able to overcome our negative fears.

Let's keep in mind, a fraction of that time, we've had to deal
    with Donald Trump;
To put it all in the right perspective, he's just our country's
    minor slump.
He should be treated like he's a virus; bacteria or bad germ in
    our midst.
And we're the right type of disinfectant or antiviral antidote to
    extinguish him, so he'd no longer exist.
Looking at the big picture, our country's future still can be
    bright.
Getting rid of Trump and Trumpism is the focus; we must never
    give up the fight.
Let's build on our future towards giving us that shot;
If we focus with that mindset, there's a better chance than not.

That big picture is definitely our answer, adding to everything
    we've already got.

The January 6 committee has probed deeply into the investigation:
Their overall findings determined there was no election fraud in
    that entire situation,
Proving Trump's allegations are all made-up lies, fake news, and
    untruths;
The real information has been thoroughly documented using all
    the known, obvious proof.
The nut jobs around Trump, some are afraid and are bailing out;
His backups and loyalists' numbers are weaning, statistics show
    there's no doubt.

Trump keeps hollering, "I can't get any justice!" This we know
    is a lie every time he opens his mouth, and it doesn't ever
    make you wonder why,

Come on, everybody; let's look at all the conclusive evidence:
Donald Trump's preposterous lies and fake news are really quite
    prevalent.
The number of people behind him seems to now have slowly
    swollen;
If things keep moving in the direction they want, the 2024 elec-
    tion could be stolen.

PRESIDENT #45 PROVEN UNWORTHY!

It's been all on the news, which is really great:

Trump's closer to criminal charges; there's still determining the
    dates.

It's definitely going to happen in three places;

This is all just the beginning of many more cases.

When all the evidence is exposed, it's going to get very bumpy;

It's going to make all his supporters very upset and grumpy.

It's all just around the corner, and has been coming for quite
    some time;

All America will finally see evidence of all his negative slime.

Talk is cheap; the proof will come out, so clean out your ears.

We'll finally know what Trump did while in office during his
    four presidential years.

We'll understand his evil plans; they'll all come to light.

The bottom line: We'll know all his crimes, proving he's not at
    all real bright.

Trump says he's the very best,

Yet completely failing all his big tests.

He's not commenting on those bad outcomes;

Starting on day one, he pointed fingers, blaming everyone.

When he was put to the task and under the gun,

When what he was doing ended, it wasn't any fun.

All presidents take an oath to serve, protect, and defend;

Donald Trump was the first to break that sacred trend.
What will he do next? What should we expect?

His track record shows that's a secret only he really knows.
All he's focused on is just implementing evil deeds;
They won't be something good, even though it should
Be something our country desperately really needs.
While he was in office, Trump continually let our country down,
Making important decisions haphazardly ended up to be unsound.
We hope the Trump era is over and never will we experience it
    again;
Everything should stay shut down to bring all his madness to an
    end.

IT'S LOOKING LIKE TRUMP IS DONE!

Trump's friends and supporters who are state level political occupants

Were identified as people who submitted fraudulent official electoral documents;

They thought the scheme was untraceable and definitely wouldn't be seen,

Thinking they would not get caught and would get away clean.

It was a very underhanded, vicious plot.

After intense investigation and scrutiny, this ugly scheme was stopped.

They wanted to illegally overturn the election, saying Trump won over Biden,

Declaring Donald Trump would be the victor and would easily slide in.

Thank GOD their schemed conspiracy was caught and didn't work,

Exposing all those cheating, lowlife, scheming, negative jerks!

This was discovered as the underhanded latest, and it's really nothing new;

Showing how scandals have spread down to state levels, it's what is now true.

They tried to submit phony electoral votes and were exposed as fake;

Trying to re-elect Donald Trump that way was definitely at
    stake.
All the evidence against Trump is near and almost complete;
These facts are all out in the open and never were discreet.
The majority of the country like and accept the truth and are
    aware;
However, Trump's gang thinks otherwise—whatever he does is
    always fair.
They'll go down kicking, screaming, and swinging, always put-
    ting up a big fight.
No matter what's proven the truth to them, they'll say it's all
    lies and not right,
Some people don't know the difference between made up truth
    and a lie.
So what's the use convincing them? We might as well not even try.
It's obvious to us and known, Trump definitely has shown,
His main focus, objective, and endeavor,
Is to change our system of democracy forever.

This fight to preserve our democracy since Trump has really
    been heated;
His ultimate goal and objective is to completely defeat it.
How much more lunacy does Trump actually show is on his mind?
We continually go through this same thing, time after time.
Enough—no more! It's time to stop this ugly total score.
I'm not sure how we can close and do it,
But we can no longer continually go through it.

TRUMP'S NEGATIVITY KEEPS CLIMBING!

The insurrection was completely preplanned by Trump and his
cronies;
What was done was deadly serious and was definitely not
phony.
Those planners are upset it didn't succeed and however failed;
Hundreds of those rioters are being caught and are ending up
going to jail.
It's really quite odd, crazy, and upsetting; those people thought
they were doing right,
Attacking the government by going to the Capitol and creating
an antigovernment, big fight.
The bottom line of what they did was against our American tra-
ditions:
Under all circumstance right or wrong, and all intervening con-
ditions,
If this was in a war, they'd be found guilty and shot by a firing
squad;
That would've been done as normal procedure and not at all
seen as odd.
What Trump represents is not something that is considered
really great;
Does nothing but divide the country and only promotes divisive
hate.

Trump's proven to be a racist, many times over long before;

This has been written about him so often, it definitely can't be
ignored.

He has no compassionate perceptions; or maybe he just doesn't
care.

People whom are in dire need of help, he definitely just
wouldn't dare.

There's a large number of Americans in our country who think
the same way as him;

It all means a portion of the country's mentality is very, very grim.

Looking out for and doing good for people of color isn't really
Trump's "A game";

Being evil, nasty, and negative is more to his claim to fame.

Using these descriptions are the definitions of this very unpleas-
ant man

Who's never ever been good for America; that's what we do un-
derstand.

He's encroached on some people's humanity and has done this
again time after time,

His compassion for all people is something commonly none
know as being quite benign,

To a lot of people, he's thought of as "the Boogieman," and
they are really scared.

When the 2024 general election comes around, we all must do
the right things and be well prepared.

DONALD TRUMP & NASTY FLIES

Donald Trump and nasty flies…**<u>I really do despise.</u>**

<u>WHY?</u> Because flies are nasty…and Donald Trump **<u>TELLS BIG LIES</u>** (OVER 16,240).

<u>PLUS,</u> he always plays head games to **<u>PULL THE WOOL OVER OUR EYES,</u>**

Tries to psych people's minds on a **<u>TWISTED FANTASY RIDE.</u>**

<u>He CHEATS, FRONTS, and SCHEMES, and WILL NEVER ADMIT WHY;</u>

<u>Creates evil plans</u> to be **<u>SNEAKY,</u>** that's what **<u>HE ALWAYS TRIES.</u>**

Trump's **<u>thinking and decision making is TOTALLY OFF TRACK;</u>**

<u>The RESULTS of his time in office reveals COMPLETELY all THESE FACTS.</u>

The majority of his statements usually end up **<u>BEING WRONG;</u>**

What comes out of his mouth whenever he talks is his **<u>SAME UNTRUTHFUL SONG.</u>**

Complains of **<u>"Witch Hunts, Fake News, etc."</u>** to deflect and defy.

Watch out when he plays nice guy, **<u>HIS SLIME HE TRIES TO HIDE.</u>**

Evidently, it's well known his **TALK IS WAY OUT OF WHACK,**

And all **Trump lovers** need to realize, it's just more **NEGATIVE FACTS.**

Says **B.S.** and causes problems at the blink of an eye,

He's a **backstabber, backslider, never caring about image or pride.**

Now…what's just been said about him **can't** be denied;

So…if you're **choosing between those two,**

Donald Trump…Or nasty flies,

We know he will **NEVER SPEAK ANY TRUTH,**

So it's **BEST** to take the **NASTY FLIES!**

THE TRUTH ABOUT TRUMP

Whenever Trump makes a wild **<u>BOGUS LIE</u>** and claim,
The results end up being exactly the same:
Whatever's been said is **<u>outrageously lame.</u>**

It's evident no one's remotely surprised,
Just adds to the total of his **<u>BIZARRE LIES</u>** (over 16,240).

He claims "Fake News, Witch Hunts, Hoaxes, and
Frauds" are the case;
He says, "It's what **<u>Americans will foolishly embrace.</u>**"

There's no mistake; **<u>NO</u>** truth will he **<u>ever speak.</u>**
He thinks we're all **<u>SUCKERS, really STUPID and WEAK,</u>**
Trump's shown he's **<u>never, ever</u>** going to change,
Always pointing fingers and saying, **<u>"I'M NOT TO BLAME!"</u>**
He's **<u>coldblooded</u>** and shows **<u>no shame to his game.</u>**

Now…we've known all these facts about him from the **<u>start,</u>**
He's proven and shown he has **<u>NO COMPASSIONATE
HEART.</u>**
And…**<u>ON TOP OF IT ALL…THE MAN'S NOT AT ALL
SMART.</u>**

So…the bottom line and great news we're happy to know:
Donald Trump's **<u>BEEN IMPEACHED,</u>** *and in November…the*
<u>*SLIME BALL HAS GOTTA GO!*</u>

MORE TRUTH ABOUT TRUMP

America's facing a serious <u>CRISIS</u>…sadly, in this <u>day and age,</u>
Because the president's leadership <u>is a **PROVEN OUTRAGE.**</u>
<u>He's also the reason why we're living in such a dangerous time.</u>
<u>Trump **REALLY THINKS HE'S ABOVE THE LAW**</u>
<u>AND **CAN** commit **ANY** crime.</u>

His party in the House and Senate <u>**can't make any decisions on**</u>
  <u>**their own;**</u>
It's like <u>**they're young children growing, but not yet fully grown,**</u>
<u>**And Trump oversees them, like he's their KING on a throne.**</u>
Trump's definitely a bona fide <u>**EGOMANIAC;**</u>
<u>**All evidence proves that is a FACT,**</u>
And it's the reason why our country is so far <u>**OFF TRACK.**</u>
Where did his negativity originate and begin
For him to be such an <u>**ADULT**</u> who's <u>**TOTALLY UNHINGED?**</u>
It must've started when he was a child,
Doing <u>**WHATEVER HE WANTED, and NOW RUNNING**</u>
  <u>**COMPLETELY WILD!**</u>

Our country needs <u>**a major change, especially at the top;**</u>
If that doesn't happen, <u>**he'll continue to feel he can't be stopped.**</u>
The <u>**B.S.**</u> Trump says and does is <u>**WAY FAR TOO MUCH;**</u>
We've had more than our <u>**SHARE of him—NO MORE!**</u> We've

had **enough!**

Add to that, his stupid mess, and the rest of his CRAZY STUFF,

Everything he says is usually **BIG FAT NASTY LIES** (over

    16,240);

Proves he's **UNTRUSTWORTHY,** a **REAL SLIME BALL,** and

    a **COLDBLOODED, RACIST…BIGOTED GUY!**

THE DONALD TRUMP DEFECT-AFFECT

Trump's <u>VIOLATED his OATH of OFFICE</u>

And <u>FAILED "The Allegiance to Our Flag."</u>

<u>He's NOT supported liberty and justice for all;</u>

What he's done and doing is really bad.

<u>Republicans are in favor of his actions;</u>

 They say he's performing real great.

So what does this mean for us regular people?

<u>IT'S NOTHING AT ALL IN THE United States.</u>

The direction and future we're leading to is a <u>real dark and ugly</u>

   <u>fate;</u>

SO, who's responsible for this DIRECTION?

<u>DONALD TRUMP…from his election TO THIS PRESENT</u>

   <u>DATE.</u>

The framers knew a time could come when the <u>president is</u>

   <u>grossly incorrect;</u>

When that time comes, it's the people's job to <u>vote and totally</u>

   <u>reject.</u>

Day after day, month after month,

Who's the <u>BIG FAT LIAR</u>…? <u>Donald John Trump</u> (over

   16,240).

Negative things are always happening, in plain sight and at

   large,

Because we have a reckless. uncaring leader who's the MAIN
MAN IN CHARGE,

OFTEN calling people dirty, nasty names; this fact we all know.

He's obviously a real lowlife person, that fact Trump always
shows.

He's positioned the American public to be DANGEROUSLY at
high risk,

Because he won't produce any positive ways and solutions to
help and assist,

And won't help the common people to move forward and be-
come self-enabled, NOT caring to bring any serious plans
of good policies to the table,

Always trying to wiggle by and sidestep our country's Constitution,

Again, not bringing forth positive ways of meaningful solutions.

Obviously, Trump's proven to be a real DISGRACEFUL, NEG-
ATIVE shame,

Constantly playing underhanded and sneaky, slimy games.

So, in November, WE HOPE WILL BE...THAT PER-
MANENT CHANGE!

UNHIDDEN TRUTH OF DONALD TRUMP

America's in a negative <u>STATE OF A GRAVE AND DIRE EMERGENCY;</u>

Things are at the point of an <u>EMINENT CRISIS and with GREAT URGENCY,</u>

Because Trump's unhinged negative <u>ABUSE OF POWER</u>

Is causing <u>MAJOR NATIONAL PROBLEMS constantly</u> by the <u>HOUR.</u>

Our country has never had <u>until now, a leader, who CANNOT LEAD;</u>

All Trump knows is <u>UNDERHANDED, DIRTY, DISGRACE-FUL DEEDS.</u>

<u>WE NEED A POSITIVE CHANGE OPPOSITE THE DIREC-TION THE COUNTRY'S BEING RUN;</u>

Without question, something <u>MAJOR...needs and HAS GOT TO BE DONE!</u>

There's an <u>AUTHORITARIAN MONSTER currently in CHARGE,</u>

<u>WREAKING HAVOC ON OUR SOCIETY IN PLAIN SIGHT AND definitely, AT LARGE.</u>

<u>TRUMP'S MADNESS REALLY NEEDS TO STOP... A.S.A.P...TODAY.</u>

What more can be said about him...? <u>WHAT MORE CAN I SAY?</u>

His ACTIONS HAVE PROVEN to be DANGEROUSLY CON-
TAGIOUS;

With his approval, REPUBLICANS IN CONGRESS HAVE ALSO BECOME OUTRAGEOUS,

DONALD TRUMP MUST BE STOPPED AT ALL COST;

We don't need a LOWLIFE BIGOT being AMERICA'S BOSS!

America has been strongly established for over hundreds of years;

Trump has eroded that establishment in just over THREE short YEARS

And has BROUGHT ABOUT people's DEEPEST and DARKEST FEARS.

Trump's time in office shows the EVIDENCE, and it's more than ENOUGH

To know, we don't need any more of his mess, cleaning it up is going to be REALLY TOUGH!

DONALD TRUMP: TRUTH EXPOSED

The president is **VERY HAPPY** when the country is **DIVIDED;**
 ON THE OTHER HAND, HE'S NOT SO HAPPY when
 America is united.
His **actions prove** he'd like to have **"A BANANA REPUBLIC";**
What he says and does is the proof of this and **main theme** on
 this subject.
The attorney general automatically does all TRUMP'S bidding;
The evidence proves from **BARR'S** actions…**I'm not kidding.**
All the people who like Donald Trump and **say they're on his side**
NEED TO WAKE UP…and REALIZE, HE'S PUTTING US
 ON A MAJOR DOWNSLIDE.
A SERIOUS CHANGE HAS TO COME QUICKLY before it's
 TOO LATE TO STOP AMERICA from moving **BEYOND**
 an IRREVERSIBLE FATE.
 It's really **DEADLY SERIOUS** and **BY NO MEANS IS THIS**
 GREAT.

With **investigations, indictments, and convictions of all his**
 friends
Continuing constantly, **ALL THE TIME,** it seems to **NEVER**
 END.
The TRUTH IS, they're all a BUNCH OF IDIOTS and stupid
 bungling CLOWNS.

The bottom line is, when it's **ALL OVER**, they're **ALL GOING
DOWN.**
**Our DEMOCRACY is on the line at the BALLOT BOX this
year.**
**VOTING TRUMP OUT OF OFFICE will ERASE all our
DEEPEST, DARKEST FEARS.**
His **corruption mess** we see and suffer with, **each and every day,**
Is **exhausting; we NEED a MAJORITY VOTE to make sure he
DOESN'T stay!**

TRUMP IS NOT GOOD FOR AMERICA

After a thorough assessment of the <u>president, Donald Trump,</u>
The <u>conclusion</u> is, our <u>COUNTRY'S in a MAJOR DECLINE
AND SLUMP.</u>
Looking at his accomplishments, <u>assessing his overall first term,</u>
Shows a <u>LACK OF INTELLIGENCE; that's a SERIOUSLY
HUGE CONCERN.</u>

Trump <u>TRIES constantly</u> to present his <u>FAKE and PHONY
CHARM;</u>
What this <u>ONLY does to America causes GREAT MAJOR
HARM.</u>
It's what our <u>country sees from him each and every day,</u>
Adding to the <u>TOTAL</u> evidence: <u>Trump MUST NOT STAY.</u>
The truth about him speaks <u>VOLUMES on its own and in IT-
SELF.</u>
Plainly stated, he's <u>BAD for our country's present and future
health.</u>
<u>Simply put, it's another reason why TRUMP MUST BE
STOPPED,</u>
<u>So that AMERICA can REGAIN its SOLE WORLDLY POSI-
TION...WE USED TO HAVE AT THE TOP.</u>
We need a <u>POSITIVE SURGE from the DEMOCRATIC
PARTY'S SIDE</u>

<u>To get our COUNTRY moving FORWARD again on a POSI-
TIVE STRIDE.</u>

And <u>what IS IT people DON'T like mostly about TRUMP the
man?</u>
He's <u>**NOT GOOD**</u> for the <u>COUNTRY;</u> he's just a <u>**BIG, UGLY
SHAM.**</u>
Come on America…we all have to keep in mind and <u>RE-
MEMBER:</u>
We've <u>**GOT TO GET HIM OUT OF OFFICE WHEN WE
VOTE IN NOVEMBER!**</u>

TRUMP: THE WORST PRESIDENT

With the fear of the <u>coronavirus affecting more people daily</u>
<u>and getting closer to us,</u>
Trump claims this <u>WORLD PANDEMIC "IS NOT ALL</u>
<u>THAT SERIOUS"</u>!
Adding <u>TOTAL CHAOS to the coronavirus CRISIS situation,</u>
The <u>medical experts</u> say <u>he's SPREADING false and misleading</u>
<u>information.</u>
With America facing massive <u>CONTAMINATION,</u>
<u>TRUMP'S ATTITUDE DISPLAYS a LACK of FOCUSED</u>
<u>AND SERIOUS MOTIVATION.</u>
<u>HIS ENTIRE RECORD AS PRESIDENT IS SADLY VERY</u>
<u>GRIM:</u>
He's <u>NOT ABOUT THE AMERICAN PEOPLE; HE'S ONLY</u>
<u>ABOUT HIM.</u>
He ends up always <u>DROPPING THE BALL,</u>
<u>NOT ABLE to figure out how to MAKE THE RIGHT CALLS;</u>
It's very tiring to see what Trump <u>WON'T DO.</u>
That's how he's handled <u>his office as President—it's nothing</u>
<u>NEW.</u>
The way he <u>ACTS and PERFORMS HIS JOB,</u>
It's like he's <u>WORKING for an ORGANIZATION LIKE THE</u>
<u>MOB.</u>
He has a high level of <u>NEGATIVITY,</u>

AND IT SPEAKS VOLUMES, SHOWING A ZERO LEVEL
    OF INTEGRITY.
THESE ARE NOT OVERSTATEMENTS ABOUT DONALD
    TRUMP;
IT'S JUST MOUNTAINS OF PROOF THIS MAN HAS TO
    BE DUMPED.
Citizens have TONS of regrets he was elected president.
Since he's been in office, that fact is highly SELF EVIDENT;
BEFORE THE COUNTRY CAN MOVE FURTHER
    AHEAD…IT MUST BE SAID,
WE'VE GOT TO MAKE SURE HIS RE-ELECTION BID IS
    COMPLETELY DEAD!

DONALD TRUMP: A NEGATIVE LEADER

History will show TRUMP'S negative personality and how he'll
be defined,
Being COMPLETELY THE WORST PRESIDENT OF ALL
MODERN TIMES.
That's how he'll be thought of FOREVER; that's the BOTTOM
LINE.
All the name calling he does shows he has a CHILD'S MEN-
TALITY,
Not able to communicate INTELLIGENTLY on an ADULT'S
LEVEL OF MORALITY.
He's got to be beaten WITHOUT A DOUBT in the next GEN-
ERAL election;
America CAN'T CONTINUE AT ALL in this horrible direction.
HATEFULNESS, EVILNESS, and VINDICTIVENESS is how
he performs;
Trump's MASSIVE NEGATIVITY IS WORKING AGAINST
ALL AMERICAN NORMS.
His INJUSTICES are PLAIN TO SEE and always made VERY
CLEAR,
Completely impacting the country we LOVE and HOLD VERY
DEAR.
He's doing great HARM and has put all citizens in a BAD PO-
SITION,

Because of his <u>**DECISIONS to cut IMPORTANT PROGRAMS**</u>
<u>**has put us IN BAD CONDITION.**</u>

It's going to <u>TAKE A LOT OF TIME</u> to recover <u>COM-</u>
<u>PLETELY</u> from <u>ALL OF THIS;</u>

For the <u>GOOD OF OUR COUNTRY,</u> we <u>MUST NOT LET</u>
<u>THESE THINGS CONTINUE TO PERSIST.</u>

In Trump's <u>FANTASY WORLD,</u> he thinks what <u>HE'S DOING</u>
<u>IS REALLY GREAT;</u>

Only a twisted <u>LEADER</u> would think like that, proving <u>HIS</u>
<u>MIND'S OUT IN OUTER SPACE.</u>

<u>His whole administration is really a MAJOR CLOWN SHOW.</u>

This fact is <u>DEFINITELY</u> in <u>PLAIN SIGHT, and EVERY</u>
<u>BODY OBVIOUSLY KNOWS.</u>

<u>ALL AMERICAN CITIZENS, PLEASE MARK DOWN THE</u>
<u>COMING NOVEMBER VOTING DATE,</u>

<u>WE'VE GOT TO STOP THIS IGNORANT LEADER BE-</u>
<u>FORE IT'S TOO LATE!</u>

TRUMP: THE NEGATIVE PRESIDENT

American people, PLEASE listen up and PAY CLOSE ATTEN-TION:

Trump's causing our country **GREAT HARM and DISSEN-SION.**

It was said he was **DANGEROUS from the VERY BEGIN-NING;**

That was TRUE even after he ENDED UP WINNING.

Trump lovers **REFUSED** to see it way back then,

Even though it's been **PRESENT** and a **CONSTANT TREND.**

When coronavirus was first heard of and came on the scene,

He was saying to the public, "It's really NOT that mean."

He was calling the coronavirus situation a **BIG JOKE**

And telling the media and the public it's a **Democratic HOAX.**

He had to walk that statement back; **OBVIOUSLY, IT'S A GLOBAL PANDEMIC and TOTALLY UNTRUE.**

As usual, he says **DUMB THINGS,** not having the faintest clue.

It's sad Trump **SUPPORTERS REFUSE** to see these **REAL-ITIES**

Of HIS IGNORANT APPROACHES to things CAUSING MASSIVE FATALITIES.

People are **SCARED as HELL,** thinking of his **POSSIBLE RE-ELECTION.**

<u>LOTS of HIS VOTERS HAVE MOVED AWAY from HIM,
VOTING IN THE OPPOSITE DIRECTION.</u>

In conclusion, **Democrats** are really <u>HARD AT WORK and
UNDER THE GUN,</u>

Making sure Trump <u>WON'T</u> successfully complete <u>HIS SEC-
OND TERM RUN!</u>

DONALD TRUMP: NOT A PRESIDENT

The <u>**WHOLE WORLD**</u> looks at the president, saying, "He's
<u>**NOT INTELLIGENT BY NO MEANS.**</u>"
<u>**TO ADD TO THAT SENTIMENT, HE'S LIKE A BAD**</u>
<u>**DREAM;**</u>
<u>**ALL HE THINKS ABOUT ARE REALLY HORRIBLE**</u>
<u>**SCHEMES.**</u>
How did our system end up electing <u>**SUCH A TOP BOSS,**</u>
Always putting us in <u>**BAD**</u> situations <u>**ENDING in GREAT LOSS,**</u>
<u>**TEARING OUR GOVERNMENTAL SYSTEMS APART TO**</u>
<u>**THE GROUND,**</u>
<u>**REAL QUICKLY with NO EXCEPTIONS by GREAT LEAPS**</u>
<u>**and BOUNDS?**</u>
This president is <u>**DETRIMENTAL in ALL HIS NEGOTIA-**</u>
<u>**TIONS and BAD DEALINGS;**</u>
That <u>**SENTIMENT is UNANIMOUSLY FELT**</u> in <u>**MOST**</u>
<u>**PEOPLE'S FEELINGS.**</u>
The <u>**QUARANTINES in America were started BY HIM**</u> way
<u>**too LATE,**</u>
Along with the <u>**LACK of TESTING, AMPLE SUPPLIES**</u>…should
have started at the PANDEMIC'S <u>**BEGINNING DATE.**</u>
<u>**As USUAL, TRUMP continues his normal thing of LYING,**</u>
And in the <u>**MEANTIME, HUNDREDS of PEOPLE continue**</u>
<u>**DYING.**</u>

Again, we must emphasize for <u>PEOPLE TO BE AWARE,</u>
The president, <u>DEEP DOWN IN HIS HEART, DOESN'T</u>
   <u>REALLY CARE;</u>
He wants to <u>LOOK GREAT</u> to everyone at <u>ALL TIMES,</u>
<u>AT THE SAME TIME HIDING</u> his <u>DARK and NEGATIVE</u>
   <u>INNER SIGNS.</u>
We know he's a <u>MASTER OF SLIMY, GREAT DECEPTION—</u>
<u>We CAN SEE IT; WE'RE NOT BUYING IT in the coming</u>
   <u>NOVEMBER ELECTION!</u>

TRUMP: A DANGEROUS PRESIDENT

Like the <u>coronavirus</u> plus <u>DONALD</u> <u>TRUMP,</u> we must <u>find</u>
  <u>CURES.</u>

At all cost, <u>THEY</u> must be stopped; we can <u>NO LONGER EN-</u>
  <u>DURE.</u>

He's always tweeting all the time, like a <u>LITTLE BABY CRYING,</u>

<u>While COVID-19 SADLY is continually RISING.</u>

<u>Massive amounts</u> of people <u>ARE SICK,</u> and <u>UNFORTUNATELY</u>
  <u>DYING,</u>

Trump's finally <u>being thoroughly scrutinized and under the gun;</u>

Everything's <u>BEING TOTALLY EXPOSED</u> on all <u>HE'S</u>
  <u>DOING AND DONE,</u>

There used to be a time when <u>America was thought of as being great;</u>

Nowadays <u>(BECAUSE OF TRUMP)</u> the world looks at us as
  though that statement <u>is NOW FAKE.</u>

The leader we now have has <u>TARNISHED</u> that <u>IMAGE and</u>
  <u>CLAIM;</u>

America's down from a world leader, just <u>ONLY to SHAME,</u>

He has no problem lying with a <u>SERIOUSNESS AND BEING</u>
  <u>FAKE,</u>

<u>Using extremely arrogant elegance WHEN ACTING LIKE A</u>
  <u>SNAKE.</u>

<u>ALL of Trump's SUPPORTERS</u> have been <u>TOTALLY BAM-</u>
  <u>BOOZLED,</u>

<u>BUT TO EVERYBODY ELSE, THAT'S NOTHING UN-
USUAL.</u>

Whenever he opens his slimy <u>MOUTH,</u>

Count on everything he says going <u>SOUTH,</u>

Because he's the president. I wish these statements were wrong.

However, it's the <u>UNDISPUTED TRUTH, EVERY DAY, ALL
DAY LONG.</u>

It's now the <u>PEOPLE'S JOB</u> to make all this <u>MADNESS STOP</u>

By <u>VOTING IN A NEW MASSIVE CHANGE...ESPECIALLY
AT THE TOP!</u>

DONALD TRUMP: A FAKE PRESIDENT

In early February, Trump said, "The coronavirus was the Democrats playing jokes";

As **USUAL, HE WAS WRONG,** proving his **PRESIDENCY IS A REAL BIG, FAKE HOAX,**

He always says of **HIS PERFORMANCE,** he's doing a real **GREAT JOB.**

The real evidence shows **HIS PERFORMANCE;** he's just an **IGNORANT SLOB.**

The way he's handled the COVID-19 situation's got the country in a real **BAD STATE.**

Trump always does and says those things, and **it's the opposite of GREAT.**

Trump's **COMMENTS, TALKING POINTS, LYING AND FAKES NEWS**

CONTINUE TO HARM our COUNTRY'S CITIZENS with his **OFF THE WALL VIEWS.**

To sum it all up, **INCOMPETENCE** is what **HE'S ALL ABOUT;**

It's very obvious each and every time **HE OPENS HIS SLIMY MOUTH.**

He really demonstrates a **SAD AND UGLY TREND;**

Seems to be **CONSTANTLY ONGOING AND WILL NEVER END.**

Because of Donald Trump's **POOR RESPONSE** to **THE CO-RONAVIRUS CRISIS,**

It's like we're still in a **MAJOR WAR FIGHTING ISIS.**

The general election is going to be an **UPHILL HUMP**

To move on past the **MAIN MAJOR PROBLEM** known as **DONALD J. TRUMP.**

It's now the **PEOPLE'S JOB** to make this **FOUL PROBLEM COME TO A STOP**

By making a **MASSIVE CHANGE IN THE NEXT ELEC-TION, STARTING AT THE TOP!**

TRUMP: THE INCOMPETENT LEADER

Trump's response to **Covid-19 is definitely FAR FROM GOOD…and GETTING WORSE every day;**

He needs to speed up and change his **NEGATIVE** actions and stop the slow movement and delays.

The president boasted in March, the country will be back open and to work real soon;

The medical experts are saying the opposite…maybe sometime **after June.**

Trump is history's most **CORRUPT and INCOMPETENT PRESIDENT;**

That's based on all writings of recorded evidence.

Since Trump's been in office, bad things have been building up to a head;

His beginning actions have caused people to die and **even more are now DEAD.**

In America, this type of presidency, which has never been seen or happened before,

Proves he's an **inept, incompetent leader who's ROTTEN TO THE CORE.**

HEY, TRUMP LOVERS…do you still think he's good for all of US?

He shows time and time again, he's someone **you just can't TRUST!**

Add to that, a great number of us have a **high level of disgust.**

It's a shame how he's dropped the ball on such a serious matter;

Nothing or no one in modern times can be compared to be much sadder.

Eventually coronavirus will be gone, and America will prevail.

Because of Trump's leadership, he should **really be going to JAIL.**

It's evident health experts and Trump **are not** on the same page;

That's **HORRIBLE with CORONAVIRUS soaring AT SUCH a DEADLY STAGE.**

In these times, there're Trump people who are surely his diehard fans;

They must have a problem thinking clearly with a lack of ability to understand.

The question is, why is America in this position nowadays?

Because Donald Trump doesn't want to be truthful; not in any honest way.

There's a **HUGE AMOUNT** of **incompetence in Trump's personality as a whole.**

That's why getting him out of office is the good people's **ULTIMATE GOAL!**

Keep all this in MIND when it comes to VOTING TIME… PLEASE REMEMBER in NOVEMBER!

THE TRUMP PRESIDENCY DEBACLE

The following statement is obviously CLEAR:

Trump's COVID-19 response has created massively HUGE
FEAR.

He doesn't care about people's health who are sick and dying;

You can see it in his sham talking points that only prove that
he's lying.

Why didn't people see it before but elected him to his position?

He's done the same crap all his life, leaving everything in hor-
rible condition.

Trump's patterns of name calling, hatefulness, and bigotry
makes it perfectly clear;

It's what has accelerated COVID-19 exponentially, creating na-
tionwide fear.

For a while, he was perpetuating the term "CHINESE FLU"

To stoke bigoted hatred of those people between me and you.

His daily press conferences are blown out of proportion and
wrong;

Trump does these things over and over again, every day, all day
long.

His conversations demonstrate, deep inside, he's WEAK,

Because whenever he talks to the public, there's always B.S. in
his SPEECH.

Straight TRUTH is something, from him, you'll never hear;

Everything is always blown out of proportion to be perfectly clear.

Keep in MIND; don't FORGET what MUST BE DONE in NOVEMBER.

Without delay, he can't stay…AMERICA'S GOT TO REMEMBER!

DONALD TRUMP: COMPLETELY MINDLESS

Trump says one thing, and then experts say another,

What else **<u>CRAZY</u>** is he going to say? **<u>We soon will discover.</u>**

We don't need his <u>lack</u> of action making the coronavirus
<u>BIGGER.</u>

Although he sits in the White House with **<u>his finger on the
TRIGGER,</u>**

Don't let a great response to this problem be the enemy of the
<u>GOOD,</u>

Because Trump is the leader **<u>NOT DOING WHAT HE
SHOULD.</u>**

He's responsible for the **<u>suffering and everything that's GOING
ON.</u>**

He keeps on **<u>PROMOTING ENORMOUS LIES,</u>** saying **<u>the ex-
perts are the ones who are WRONG.</u>**

In the beginning, he didn't **<u>TAKE SERIOUSLY</u>** the **<u>COVID-19
outbreak;</u>**

That action has been sadly a gravely serious **<u>BIG...MISTAKE,</u>**

<u>Displaying to the whole world, he's a **REAL BIG, STUPID
FAKE.**</u>

Trump's rich buddy and corporate cronyism is his real bad ob-
session;

His wrong thinking is...we're just headed to a moderate recession.

However, **HE'S too STUPID** to realize we're really headed to a
  MAJOR DEPRESSION;
His **LACK** of good decision making as the leader at the **TOP**
Has put the **United States of America** in a really **BAD SPOT.**

Whether you're old or young…**CORONAVIRUS CAN AF-
  FECT ANYONE.**
We must stay **FIXATED on the MAJOR job that's to be done:**
Getting Trump OUT OF OFFICE to SAVE EVERYONE!

TRUMP: A TOTAL AMERICAN FAILURE

His lack of good decision making at the <u>TOP</u>

Has put the whole country in a <u>**VERY DANGEROUS SPOT.**</u>

Because of Trump's actions, the country is <u>**SHUT DOWN;**</u>

No normal activities in all our cities and towns.

<u>**INFECTIONS and DEATH TOLLS**</u> are <u>**RISING at an ACCEL-
ERATED RATE;**</u>

No one has <u>**ANY IDEA WHEN IT WILL ALL DISSIPATE.**</u>

Trump's delayed response to **COVID-19** is <u>**responsible for mul-
tiple DEATHS;**</u>

That's his actions and how he reacts to them at <u>**HIS BEST.**</u>

When he declared a <u>**national emergency because the pandemic
had grown,**</u>

Mayors and governors are supposed to be <u>**NO LONGER ON
THEIR OWN.**</u>

These <u>**NON-ACTIONS**</u> are Donald Trump's **FAILINGS,**

And is why America is <u>**MASSIVELY AILING.**</u>

Trump's said he <u>**doesn't like and won't respond to governors in
some states;**</u>

This leaves those states **citizens vulnerable** to a real <u>**DEADLY
FATE.**</u>

That's our country's leader, making a **HUGELY HORRIBLE DECISION**,
Shows not having **COMPASSION and a LACK of RESPONSIBLE VISION**.

A good person would never attempt to do **HARM** like that,
Proving Donald Trump's persona is **nothing but DIRTY CRAP**.
Trump got into office by the **Electoral College's TAINTED score**;
If the **American people's vote had counted, he wouldn't have GOT HIS FOOT in the White House DOOR**!

TRUMP: AN EGOMANIAC PRESIDENT

Trustworthiness, honesty, are definitely **NOT TRUMP'S DE-
MEANOR;**
Our **country deserves leadership with a mentality level that's
much cleaner.**
The majority of **Americans all feel the same way,**
Proves he's the same **UNSTABLE LIAR** we've witnessed **every
single day.**
With this pandemic upon us and **TRUMP'S** the **Commander-in-
Chief,**
He's caused high anxiety **AMONG US.** and a huge feeling of
GRIEF.

Trump gets **MAD** when he's held accountable for **lies** he's pre-
viously said;
If he'd started doing right, many citizens wouldn't have
ENDED UP DEAD.
When he's criticized, he throws **TEMPER TANTRUMS, just
like a little boy,**
And treats **THE UNITED STATES of AMERICA** as if it's his
PLAY TOY.
Trump's administrative people **AREN'T ALLOWED TO
SPEAK TRUTH for FEAR of HIS FURY;**

It's common <u>HOW HE REACTS—THAT'S HIS WHOLE LIFE'S STORY.</u>

His <u>likes</u> giving <u>TAX BREAKS to his rich buddies, cronies, and HIMSELF;</u>

Does <u>NOTHING FOR REGULAR PEOPLE OR ANYBODY ELSE.</u>

There's a long list of facts, proving horrible deceit and <u>NO GOOD.</u>

All American citizens need…to reject this <u>NARCISSIST as they should.</u>

TRUMP: ALL LIES AND VOID OF THE TRUTH

It's **SHAMEFUL** for America to have a leader that's **BAD**; that's
a **FACT**.

We're hoping the voting process will stop him **<u>QUICKLY in his
TRACKS.</u>**

<u>Healthcare professionals</u> say his COVID-19 plans are inade-
quate and don't fit;

Whatever Trump focuses on is mostly **<u>NEVER SMART or LEGIT.</u>**

If only he would stop talking, saying **<u>STUPID</u>** and **<u>DUMB
THINGS;</u>**

Obviously, he's a **<u>STUPID IDIOT,</u>** not **seeing all the problems it
brings.**

Trump **<u>lies about himself, always saying, "I'M DOING A
GREAT JOB!"</u>**

Nobody believes that **<u>CRAP</u>** he talks, because it's coming from
a **<u>LYING, DUMB A SLOB.</u>**

If Trump had taken action when COVID-19 had **<u>FIRST</u>** come
to America and at that time known,

Public officials **would have prepared sooner,** and maybe slowed
the **<u>speed and growth from which it has grown.</u>**

Simply put: It's clear the **person in the White House doesn't
really care**

About the American people, being in despair.

Since he's been in office, his **administrations have run AMUCK;**
We'll be really glad WHEN HIS TIME IS FINALLY UP!

TRUMP: HISTORY'S WORST PRESIDENT

Medical professionals are saying DANGER; COVID-19 is run-
ning RED HOT.
Trump's coronavirus task force is trying to say it's really NOT.
His comments and statements all the time are widely suspect,
Because they're coming out of the mouth of a mental REJECT.

Whenever Trump makes an alleged serious suggestion,
It always steers America in the WRONG DIRECTION.
Trump would do better by keeping his mouth CLOSED;
Most times do even better by only speaking through his NOSE.
His speeches rattle on with a lot of B.S. and a bunch of nothing,
While in the meantime, LARGE NUMBERS of people continue
suffering.
It took over two months for TRUMP to acknowledge the virus
crisis,
After which front line workers and patients paid severely deadly
prices.
What's WRONG with Trump's mind?
Why didn't he start helping in time?
Towards a thorough and complete solution
To bring all this to a final conclusion,
He never works in good faith;
Chooses always to hesitate.

The country must massively organize
And no longer agonize.

TRUMP: EXPOSED THE WORST...
HANDS DOWN

It doesn't take a genius, or a rocket scientist to know,

When Trump speaks, it's **ONLY** the **Donald Trump TV show.**

He makes comments definitely showing he's really a **FOOL**

And didn't get his mindset from any **reputable school.**

IT'S—NATURAL!

Since he acknowledged COVID-19 and **hundreds of thousands**
   continue dying,

Trump's doing the same old thing...he **CONTINUES LYING.**

His press conferences are **COMPLETELY** inaccurate presentations;

He's like a **MENTAL PATIENT, NOT TAKING HIS MEDI-**
   CATIONS.

His talking points and comments, always **blown out of proportion,**

He thinks no **ONE CAN SEE** all the **OBVIOUS DISTORTIONS,**

Wants at **ASAP speed all churches on Sundays packed;**

That **DUMB CRAP he said is REALLY A FACT.**

Trump has no insight on what that negative mess will do;

PUTS EVERYONE AT HIGH RISK, including me and you.

From the beginning, **NEVER COMPREHENDING SERIOUS**
   SITUATIONS,

Acting **FOOLISH AND CRAZY,** putting **AT RISK THE EN-**
   TIRE NATION,

Knowing nothing but <u>STEEPED MASSIVE DISINFORMATION,</u>

And absolutely horrifying against the <u>BETTERMENT of OUR NATION,</u>

Trump's government is standing down on this coronavirus invasion.

What would a logical person do to stop that <u>INCORRECT EQUATION?</u>

<u>THE ANSWER IS…DUMP-TRUMP; HE'S NOTHING BUT A STINKY SKUNK!</u>

THE TRUMP ADMINISTRATION IS FOUL

The man who's the president, officials do not trust;
What he says and what he's does breeds a high level of disgust.
Trump's an evil, hateful, negative man, with no credibility;
Never presents any actions showing positive stability.
The president's priorities and track record is not based on any-
   thing in positive time;
His vision on everything is worse than a person walking around
   blind.

In all instances, Trump really doesn't know what to do;
Meaning, it's plain and simple, he doesn't have a clue!
Badly impacting our country, especially for me and you,
Clearly we're living in the darkest days in our country's history;
It's very obvious and clear—this is not even a mystery.
America's in its most negative place, more so than ever before,
Because of Donald Trump's leadership; that's a true statement
   for sure!

All Trump's administration and staff are truly his puppets;
When he's beaten out of office, they can get a job with the Muppets.
His toxic talk shows he's in a war with this pandemic's science,
Not at all working with or acknowledging with a positive ap-
   proach of compliance.

WAKE UP, EVERYBODY! NO MORE SLEEPING ON THIS THOUGHT. WE MUST THINK IT THOROUGHLY THROUGH.
Time for ACTION IS IN FRONT OF US—WE CAN SEE WHAT WE HAVE TO DO!

TRUMP'S RUNNING OUT OF TIME

Trump's proof when there's a knucklehead at the top,
Good leadership for the people will always stop;
These facts show up in everything he does and will say;
It's ongoing all the time, each and every day.

We've got to stop the madness Donald Trump projects,
Only caring about himself; everything else total neglect.
Come on, America, what more evidence do you need
To get him out of office with maximum speed?

This president is a big slime ball and a big, fat snake.
That's two of the things about him that's truly not fake.
Trump is America's psychopathic commander-in-chief;
Knowing that shows we desperately need major relief.
He's failing America on all major fronts;
That's why our country is in a major slump.
His defiance has created this massive Covid-19 spike,
And it shows us what he's doing is what he really likes.
Pence needs to find a lifeboat off the Donald Trump Titanic,
So he doesn't have to face the last minute panic.

TRUMP: THE CON-MAN IS DONE!

Because it just sticks in my mind, I'll have to say it every time,

It's evident Trump's a SUPER FOOL,

And the only platform he needs is his **toilet stool.**

Trump has always said…so it needs to be written in **red,**

When he's making his biggest lying claims,

He always says, **"I'M NOT THE BLAME."**

His lies are really an awful shame,

And it really exposes his nasty, B.S. games.

I'll say it one more time: he's really an ignorant fool;

It shows he didn't get a good education at any decent school.

In January 2020, when Covid-19 came very near,

His lack of action and stupidity became very clear.

No action from him at all showed up,

Because his non-existent brainpower was trying to play tough.

Always refusing to wear a face mask,

Because sanity indicates it's not a complicated task,

I wish he'd put a face mask on and wear it as a gag,

And keep it on all the time, so we won't have to hear the crap
    he brags!

THANK GOD—
NEVER TRUMP (WE HOPE) AGAIN!

It's the worst of the worst things Trump has ever tried,
Not acknowledging Covid-19, people dying and have died.
The massive number of fatalities, in his coldblooded view,
Thinks it's NOT that serious…knowing him, what the heck…
    that's nothing new!

Trump ignores things of importance with enormously great ease,
Shows he's a coldblooded person; never cared about this disease.
A huge failure during his term in office is what he's ever shown,
And during his term in office, this situation has only grown.

Trump's obsessed with political loyalties over smart science;
He'll blast any politian not giving him total compliance.
Putting the country on course for a political collision,
Creating massive hatred and heated widespread division,
He seems to have always done this all the time
And never stopped, thinking he'll be just fine.
Because in his mind, he's above everyone; a person who's divine.
His mind's in fantasyland, that fact is very clear.
This is nothing new; he's been that way for many, many years,
Never ever wearing a face mask, thinking he's completely immune,
Because that's what he's doing; he'll catch it <u>again</u> real soon!

So far, dumb luck is what he's really had,

When his luck runs out, it's gonna be very, very bad.

He has no sense of logic; for a president, that's a real disgrace,

Never displaying any intelligence—that's always his case.

He constantly plays ugly, nasty and dirty blame games,

Showing the more things change, the more they stay the same.

TRUMP: A FULL-BLOWN CROOK!

Trump says anybody who throws a punch at him, he throws a
    punch right back;
That's the mentality of a small-minded little boy; a real low life.
    That's a fact.
It shows the lack of intelligence in Donald Trump,
And the main reason it's about time for him to be completely
    dumped.

Never reaching out to those American people in dire need,
Always going in the opposite direction with excessive speed,
Doesn't want the public to know about all the sneaky money
    he's made,
Hiding his crookedness and nasty dirty moves hidden in the
    dark shade.

Trump's title should be called "The Toddler & Chief";
Gets angry, throws temper tantrums when anyone turns up the
    heat.
It's well-documented he was ill suited to be the president,
Because what he's done while in office is really self-evident.

His track record has shown, and he's proven to be extremely a
    racist;

It all shows up in his decision-making from all angles and bases.

Always flip-flopping on comments and in conversations,

That's real bad for a supposed leader of our nation.

What else can be said to those people who really don't believe?

Because that's all he's ever wanted to do, is divide and deceive.

DONALD TRUMP: CRIMINAL NO. #1

Trump says he won the election…we know the truth how it went;
We also know, as usual, he's lying **100 percent.**
Way back in 2016, Hilary Clinton said, **"Trump is really DAN-
GEROUS."**
It's been proven she was completely right, and he is completely
BRAINLESS.
Adding to that Trump's hypocrisy
Is a gravely dark stain on American democracy.

As a person, he's completely **EVIL** minded,
Never showing an ounce of human kindness,
Completely **ROTTEN** to the core;
America can no longer take it anymore.

When you think of it…it's just so, so sad,
And add in his THUG supporters, that's just really, really super
bad.
This has really been evident for the past four years.
Finally now showing up, bringing to light all of our darkest fears,
Never ever has there been a leader this far from being good.
Now everyone can really see it, and it's clearly understood.

TRUMP: OUR COUNTRY'S DISGRACE!

For the past four years, our democracy's been under assault;
We know who's to blame for that: it's Donald Trump's fault.
Millions of misinformed people voted on his side,
But at the ballot box, this time, his second term's been denied.
Thank God the majority of voters' decision turned out right,
And now after all this time, he continues to put up a fight.

All the country now can see Trump's really off the hook,
And it really has exposed him to be a dirty nasty crook.
Some of us knew this from his very beginning,
Even though he says he always ends up winning.

Trump's second impeachment will be the first time in our country's history;
For all the corrupt things he's committed in life, it's not even a mystery.
He'll never be in politics again (I HOPE) and can't hold any high public job;
The only thing left for him is to create another dangerous mob.
All the things he's done in life, he's always messed up.
Since he's out of office now, all those things will finally catch up!

TRUMP/TERRORISTIC PRESIDENT

White supremacists and Donald Trump are all on the same side,
And obviously in plain sight, they're not even trying to hide.
Their goal is creating a political diversion and deflection,
To undermine the facts of free and fair elections.
The evidence shows he will cheat; that's what he'll do,
Perform his shenanigans and think he didn't leave a clue.

A majority of Republicans still stick with him, trying to be discreet;
They won't stop what they're doing until America turns up the
    heat.
If he'd won the election, the country would really be in super
    bad shape,
Even worse than when Nixon tried to hide Watergate.

The Biden administration's job will be getting the country back
    on track;
It'll take a real long time for them to clean up Trump's insane acts.
Trump's mentally unfit, as everybody can plainly see;
Only his MAGA crowd's on his side—they will completely disagree.
When he's out of office, his legal problems will grow and even-
    tually prevail;
He'll end up wearing a prisoner's jumpsuit and sitting in some
    lonely jail.

TRUMP: NO LONGER OUR PROBLEM!

Trump's the country's lead white-supremacist-in-chief;

He's finally been stopped—now we'll get needed relief!

He's been impeached again. That's super **<u>GOOD NEWS.</u>**

Next should be more of **<u>his republicans,</u>** like Ted Cruz.

A lot of people around him have left in disgust;

They don't want to be next to be thrown under the bus.

His financial assets are gonna be gone and out the door,

Because his business connections are dying, that's for sure.

The insurrection Trump caused was totally disgraceful,

Shows how deeply awful this man is—very nasty and hateful.

He's got to be held accountable for all that he's done,

Worse than a criminal holding you up using a gun!

Whoever thought in America, things would be this bad,

All because of Trump and his enablers? That's really sad.

He's mentally unstable and should be watched like a child;

What he's capable of doing could really be dangerous and wild.

The good news and bottom line is, after he's gone,

It'll feel like a new day every day, like when the sun raises at

    dawn!

NEW LIFE AFTER TRUMP!

This is what should be said that's completely on the level:

There's no question, Donald Trump is clearly nothing but the

    <u>DEVIL!</u>

He's been evil all his life, especially since being president,

Not caring what he says or does; that's what's evident.

Hatred and lies, that's all he speaks.

Anybody who's not like him, he calls them stupid and weak.

Glad all his negativeness as president has come to a final end,

President Biden's getting on a fast track towards a positive trend.

Let's let it be known and clearly understood:

Our country has seen the last of Trump—hopefully for good!

His corruption's been in our face and practiced openly and on-

    going;

This is how he's always been and what he's always been showing.

There's one major thing Americans really can't stand:

A leader who's definitely a big liar, a bigot, and a hateful

    nasty man.

For the past four years in the White House, there were total de-

    ceptions.

Thank God things have change and are now moving in the right

    direction.

Now's the time to clean up America, knowing Trump was com-
pletely wrong;
Doing just that, I know we'll come back focused and really
strong.

Things are looking positive for America and finally moving that
way for us;
We know now to never again elect someone we definitely can't
trust.
The election has shown democracy tends to always prevail,
And a person like Donald Trump will probably end up in jail!

By Winston Matubey

TRUTH ABOUT THE EX-PRESIDENT

There're a lot in the details that've brought us to this very im-
portant conclusion,
Definitely none of which is fake or a phony illusion.
This is Donald Trump's M.O., as we've always proclaimed;
What's been said is just a repeated continuation of exactly the
same.
Trump is clearly a **<u>NUT JOB;</u>**
His friends, cronies, and MAGA crowd treat him as though he's
a heart throb.
He wants the keys again to the White House door,
Hoping he'll get them back in 2024;
We've got to reject that move at all costs,
Making definitely for sure he'll never again be the leader and boss.
When he lost, he acted like a little boy
Who was separated from his most favorite toy
That always gave him great joy.
Never giving the people the feeling of being protected,
Just showing great distain and completely disrespected,
Trump's request not to show his records was denied,
Proving what he's done (all bad), he's trying to hide.
This is something a lot of us already knew;
The people behind obviously bamboozled and still don't have a
clue,

All the people not under his spell know exactly what to do.

Get it completely done, and we're under the gun, so no more
    can he run—

Stopping him is going to be really great fun.

A POEM: THE FORMER PRESIDENT/VICE PRESIDENT CONNECTION;

During that time (2016 to 2020), I just couldn't get it out of my
    head;
It's kind of an important thing to know, and really must be said:
"Donald Trump and Mike Pence are definitely joined at the hip,
Because anytime when Donald Trump had to fart,
Mike Pence had to take a S**T"!

Nothing's changed between those two, even now in this very day;
Mike Pence still has a brown nose that seems won't ever be
    going away!

You can add his republican friends to this fact,
Assuming their reputations will always be intact,
But really, their reputations are tarnished forever and never
    coming back,
Thinking Trump's actions, will keep them immune.
But when legal charges come down on them,
I hope it should finally change their tune;
Hard-headed, stupid, and not caring about us is who they really
    are—
The same mind set as Donald Trump shows up every time,
    clearly by far.

You know, I've got to say it, and it must be said just one more

    time:
Getting away from Trump after four years must have come

    from somewhere
I'd consider being divine.

A GOOD PRESIDENT IS FINALLY IN PLACE!

Donald J. Trump is finally… **<u>NO LONGER AT THE TOP!</u>**

The past four years of his B.S. lies have **<u>FINALLY BEEN STOPPED!</u>**

Joe Biden is showing he's a better man as our country's **<u>NEW president;</u>**

This fact is definitely quite obvious and clearly quite evident.

He's showing America what he's doing is what we all desperately need,

Making really good changes and decisions, ensuring the country will succeed,

And…not wasting time doing all this and moving at rapid speed.

The country is now more stable again with Joe in the Oval Office,

Reaching out to the Republicans and Democrats and working along with both caucuses,

Getting the country completely vaccinated and the economy in the right direction,

Working on all major issues and goals, first focusing on eradicating Covid's deadly infection.

He knows these issues are very important and seriously very true;

They should've been completed long ago, because we know they're really not new.

All the things Joe Biden's doing are needed and definitely right,
Ensuring America will win in everything and never lose any
    fight.

Our country's now in a better place, and really, <u>**THANK GOD
    FOR THAT.**</u>
No more of Trump's cheating and lying shenanigans and all his
    dirty, negative crap.
Joe Biden's presidency so far is looking really great;
He's being truthful and honest, staying on track, and dedicated
    to erasing ugly racial hate.

By Winston Matumbey

JOE BIDEN: THE RIGHT PRESIDENT!

Now that Joe Biden's in control,

Stopping COVID-19 is one of his main goals.

It's a shame Republicans want to keep up all their ugly fights;

Bottom line turns out what they're doing just ain't right.

All their lies, shenanigans, and playing political games;

Always end up doing nothing and saying exactly the same.

Joe's focus is on climate change, infrastructure, and many more
issues that need to be done;

He's working furiously to complete these issues and is over-
whelmingly under the gun,

Focused on bringing America back in the worldview of again
being number one,

Reversing all the negativity Mr. Donald Trump and his cronies
had previously done.

To sums it all up, nothing more needs to and can be said;

It's time to get moving and bring America back from being con-
sidered as almost dead.

By Winston Matumbey

<u>A Republican footnote:</u> Senator Tim Scott; Uncle Tim is Uncle
Tom and playing a game
of political ping-pong! (The <u>only</u> African American Republican
Senator)

AFTER ONE TERM, TRUMP WAS DUMPED

This title really says it all.
Because what he did while in office
Obviously added up to know he would fall,
He lied and said the election was a cheat;
That proved he's nothing but a dirty old creep.

All Republicans continue to follow his lead,
Doing everything to execute all his dirty deeds.
We're witnessing democracy at its very worst,
Living through a time period of an evil curse.

Trump's followers really love him and totally adore,
Thinking he'll be back in the White House in 2024.
However, there's one thing we must never ignore:
Donald Trump will always be completely rotten to the core.

If you can't see this in these days and times,
You're walking around through life being totally blind.

THE TRUMP LEGACY...FOREVER

The beauty of complete humanity does not come from this man;
Hatred and negativity is all that's shown in his plan.
From the start of the Trump presidency, we seemed to hear
Everything producing America's deepest dark and ugly fears.

It's horrible we're still exposed to that mentality all the time;
What he's done and continues doing to us should be doc-
    umented as a major crime.
Trump's an EVIL MAN
Who tried to implement his EVIL PLAN.

So what the country must do
Is make sure we'll never go through
This same awfully nasty trend,
And make sure it's totally come to the end.

TRUMP: THE ONLY HORRIBLE PRESIDENT!

Trump, his senators, and Congress-people are defiant to the rule of law.

What's wrong with their sense of decency? Do they really want our democracy to fall?

It seems as though they have a problem speaking the truth;

This is confusing for a lot of people, especially for our youth.

What Trump's planning in the future is multiple large demonstrations;

He's heating up his followers to execute real violent confrontations,

Proving he's sick, and will drive people toward doing the absolute worst,

And will go to any lengths, just to quell his evil vindictive thirst.

Since Trump's been out of office, he's still spreads disinformation, chaos, and lies;

He's really always been that way—he's that kind of a guy.

Seems he likes to see the country doing poorly, going aimlessly in different ways.

He focuses on hate and division; for him that's a real great day.

Treating all people fairly and right is against his ego and grain;

That in itself definitely proves he's utterly insane.

When he's at his M.A.G.A. rallies, he goes into long sessions of B.S., and he gloats.

The dummy doesn't realize he's the punch line for intelligent-
minded folks.
In 2016, when he got into office, we realized he was the wrong
selection;
When 2020 rolled around, we changed that problem and made
the right correction.
History in the future will record Trump as a bigot and racist;
We had to deal with him for a time, as he created a lot of racial
cases.
Trump wasn't beyond us to realize his ulterior motives;
He demonstrated and displayed his real intent when he became
the POTUS.

TRUMP: THE EPITOME OF HORRIFIC EVIL!

When GOD was giving out brains,

Trump misunderstood and thought it was a train.

Obviously, he was late to get what he got;

Being the person he is, that really says a lot.

Anybody who wants to get on the Trump train,

There's really nothing there positive and definitely nothing to gain—

You'll only be teaming up with someone who's utterly insane.

The evidence and truth speaks for itself;

The one and only thing Trump generates is poor mental health.

Temper tantrums, vindictiveness, and vengeance are definitely
his thing.

He doesn't have the capability for anything else, other than
more negativity; that's what he always brings.

I wish there were positive things to say, possibly to show that
I'm wrong,

But Trump's like an old, scratched-up, broken record, always
spouting out that same old, stupid song.

What in the world to stop him completely can we do?

THE ANSWER: All good citizens have to go out in droves,
huge masses, and vote, showing Trump, with us he's-com-
pletely-through.

We've got to speak up speak out loudly, and really make it per-
fectly clear.

We're not going to take anymore B.S. from him; we've had
    enough for more than four years.
The handwriting's in plain sight and on the proverbial, big wall.
We've got to show strength and vote forcefully at the polls in
    the fall.
On January 6, 2021, Donald Trump tried to execute, a historic
    coup;
Shows he was sloppy, drunk on power and thought; he could
    get his cheating sliminess through.
That's how badly he wanted to be the leader again; that was his
    mission to do.
He was unsuccessful—you can't say he didn't really try,
Still preaching, "THE ELECTION WAS STOLEN!" and of
    course, that's really a big, fat lie.
Because we already know who he is and no one anywhere
    wonders why,
As I've always said, "He's really that kind of a guy."
He'll exploit all avenues he can, to create for himself, complete
    insulation,
So he won't be connected to or with any type of major investi-
    gations, Trump surely doesn't want to be involved with any
    more high-level legal litigations.
Trump's political party is currently on thin ice and on very
    shaky ground,
Starting at the top and working its way to the bottom slowly, all
    the way down.

THE TRUMP TRAIN IS DOOMED TO FAIL!

Trump's proven he's an enemy of our Constitutional order;

He likes world authoritarian leaders in other lands far from our
borders.

He'd like to control our country using an iron hand;

That's something Republicans turn away from and bury their
heads in the sand.

They're not on board to do what's best for our country, way
offline;

To straighten out all our problems it's going to take a lot of time.

Before we get it turned around, there'll be a lot of political op-
position

From all those cheating, underhanded, dirty and slimy Trump
politicians.

After hearing the crazy rhetoric in all Trump's speeches,

There's only one thing left that his phony B.S. teaches,

The older he gets, nothing's changed, and his mind is already set,

To being a nasty, evil, racist, who totally likes division.

The only one place Trump should be is locked up in any prison.

There's no doubt what Trump's really about, and that's crim-
inality for sure,

Using that mentality on the masses and the downtrodden poor.

As far as he's concerned, fairness and honesty are things way in
the past;

How he feels about racism and hatred is ongoing and will
    forever last.
A multi-racial society is definitely not on his mind or in his vision;
That's the bottom line that makes up all his final decisions.
In the beginning, he said, "Mexicans are nothing but rapists,
    killers, peasants, and thieves";
He's really serious it's what he honestly believes.
The negative path Trump always takes, he won't be able to endure;
What he doesn't know, goodness is the right road, that's for sure.
It was GOD looking out for us and made sure he wasn't re-
    elected,
His M.A.G.A. crowd and fake news supporters and the ones
    who didn't accept it,
We've got GOD on our side, and behind us, we'll win; GOD
    never fails,
Those bigots and race haters who are sticking with Trump, I
    hope they eventually end up in jail.
The more Trump squeals like a pig with many different crazy
    rhetorics
Demonstrates his lack of knowledge about fundamental politics.
This shows clearly he has no knowledge about logical do's or
    don'ts;
It's why his decision making is real shaky; no one really knows
    for sure anything, if he will or if he won't.

TRUMP IS GONE BUT THE WORST GOES ON!

From the Trump presidential era, his main influences are la-
  beled "Trumpism," "Trumpian," or his cult, with all other
  ideologies—bottom-line, it's all bad.
Whatever which way you call them, there're all very ugly, nasty,
and quite sad.
All of so-called KING Trump's close people and supporters
  have been and are being subpoenaed;
The January 6 committee is very serious about the known ev-
  idence and do really mean it.
When those persons testify, let's see what they honestly, if pos-
  sible, will come clean and say;
Whatever statements they make will be very event-filled days.
Incivility was definitely proven, that's what the Trump crowds
  are all about;
Hatred and violent actions while screaming, "Stolen election!"
  is what was said during their unruly shouts.
The Republican cult side of our government is way beyond re-
  proach;
What there're doing to and in our country is un-American; they
  are bad and nasty folks.
What was just said is serious and by no means a really bad joke;
He's always lying all the time and always says he's number one.
You can always count on him saying that, just like the rising sun.

A large portion of Republicans are now following the model
Trump cult;

That explains the January 6, 2021, attack on the Capitol was a
real serious and violent assault.

Everything he's done wrong is not hidden but clearly out front,

And the main problem and person we're facing, that person's
name is Donald J. Trump.

This is the reality we're living in these horrible days and times;

Trump goes around acting and thinking he's better than every-
one else, because in his mind, he's divine,

In 2016, Trump said, "I alone can fix it!" when he started his
political career.

The only things he accomplished doing was creating violence,
corruption, hatred, and bringing on massive fear.

WITH TRUMP;
EVILNESS & LIES STILL LINGER!

When Trump was in office, he tore up, mutilated, burned, and
    flushed in the toilet official top-secret information;
He doesn't care and won't adhere to all the laws of our great
    nation.
A person like that, is definitely full of crap.
When you're the top man of the nation, you should automati-
    cally honor all laws and not create any investigations;
On the other hand, from the start of his presidency up until this
    date,
The M.A.G.A. crowd has thought Trump's always been excep-
    tional and great.
Whatever happens concerning Trump, they really don't care;
They think everything he does is correct and always fair.
One of GOD'S divine teachings is the truth is always the light,
But with Trump, nothing is right, so he'll always put up a fight.
Honest citizens are asked to always have a sense of decency and
    decorum;
That's presently not happening in our country's toxic political
    forum.
All of Trump's life, he's always told everyone around him exag-
    geratedly big lies;
It's as true as the nose on your face and the bright blue sky.

And if it's not in Trump's best interest, he'll always angrily deny.

When Trump says anything, his fans and supporters will hands-
down, whole heartedly believe;

They're completely blind to true facts, and that makes them vul-
nerable to be deceived.

Speaking truth has always been thought of as top priority, and
being absolutely supreme,

With Donald Trump's twisted mind, he has no idea what that
truly means.

All evidence and charges against him are factual and absolutely
correct;

That doesn't matter to his fan base—all decisions against him,
they'll never accept.

Because in their minds, talking bad about Trump is wrong, and
they will always reject.

The old school saying is: "You can lead a horse to water, but
you can't make him drink,"

Proving all Trump supporters will always think what they want
to think.

TRUMP: A PERSON OF TOTAL HORROR!

Trump and his close people were concluded to be highly involved

In the January 6, 2021, riot, and it's still not completely solved.

He's clearly one of the masters of chaos and disinformation—

That's really a horrible label to have, being a former leader of

    our nation.

He's the only former president to have that label, but it doesn't

    faze him one bit.

This proves he's never had the character to be a president, and

    he always thinks his mentality is legit.

The bottom line—it's been said many times—he's always been

    unfit;

During his term, when national crisis happened and needed to

    be handled,

The only thing he had time for was dealing with his many scandals,

He's the only president to be in that class all by himself, alone;

That's never before happened in history, and he did it on his own.

When important decisions and other matters were serious and

    at stake,

What he was efficient at was calling most of those situations fake.

He wants to try and make a run to come back in 2024;

We've got to see that never happens—we must work hard at it,

    definitely for sure!

Voting against him in large numbers is what we must do,

So he can't claim he was cheated and try to create another pos-
sible coup.

That type of plan could quite possibly be on top of Trump's
strategy table.

He's definitely the kind of person, who's quite willing and able.

All these negative scenarios about him can go on and on and on…

All things negative about him are possible; nothing would be
wrong.

Knowing Trump's overall nature, we must be prepared for ev-
erything.

Disruption and chaos is totally what he's capable of; it's what
he'd probably bring.

I wonder what his next move is; it's probably something crazy;

When Trump wants to do something destructive, he's definitely
not lazy!

Trump's always said, "I'm a winner, not a loser!"

Proving he talks more junk than a stink-in drunk who's a real
heavy boozer.

Some call his operation a "Three Ring Circus," and that can be so;

When you see what he always does, it's always a crazy, topsy-
turvy show.

TRUMP'S UGLY END IS NEARING!

There's a mountain of evidence about Trump's doings and
    what's been done.
How dare he think we're stupid enough to accept him, saying
    he's used good judgment while being under the gun.
We know most people he's dealt with, there has been fraudu-
    lence committed on a large scale;
All the evidence compiled proves he should really be going to jail.
Nothing's ever positive about him; what he does is constantly
    fail.
His close associates will also be going to jail—
They better straighten up and fly right,
Or they'll be locked up and won't know what's going on day or
    night,
And it'll be a long time before seeing any signs of outside de-
    lights.
They've got to be saying to themselves, "It's time to come clean
    and tell what we know."
The longer they wait, it'll worsen their fate; and bad situations
    will ultimately grow.
Those loyal to Trump could, at any time, be dumped; it's one of
    his routine goals/
It'll be all in the news; they've all gone down the tubes, like
    some of his real estate properties he's sold.

And to those African American supporters, you'll be first to be
      dumped,
Because what you'll be seeing is classic Donald Trump.
When you're done and he can't use or need you anymore,
You'll be thrown under the bus, that's for sure.
You'll be singled out as a disgrace to your race,
So think carefully and seriously what you claim and do.
Within your community, you'll definitely be through.
On top of all that messed up bunch of crap,
There'll be nowhere or way to recover or adapt.
You won't be able to play it down;
People will just look at you, shrug, and frown.
Bottom line—there'll be no coming back.
So it's best to think about getting on the right track
And get away from him ASAP from now on.
With all of his problems, his demise will be ugly, and he'll be gone.
Trump pulled the "race card" on the attorney general of the
      state of New York recently;
As we've said all along, Trump, to some people, never shows decency.
Lately his taxes have become the focus with a lot of serious
      questions;
The IRS knows what they're doing, and they're going to have
      many very scrutinizing sessions.
Afterwards, the whole Trump clan will be making some very se-
      rious confessions.
Whatever the outcome and the government decides what to do,
Definitely for sure, Trump and his family won't be able to sue.

TRUMP'S SNATCHED HIS PLACE IN HELL!

In the news (as usual), there are stories of laws Trump uncar-
ingly broke;
It's the same as usual and no new news for us honest and decent
folks.
Also it's getting worse than what we know of him from pre-
vious situations before;
It's happened so many times, you just can't keep up with the
total score.
Trump's on record to be one of history's leading nastiest, ugliest
people;
There's not too many who's on that list...there's only a few who
are equal.
Saying nasty things, when he rallied against Hilary Clinton, she
should be locked up for,
He turns around and does similar things largely and enor-
mously; much, much more.
He's being sued by multiple people, simultaneously at the same
time;
He then has the nerve to come out and say he's never com-
mitted any crimes.
Trump has a negative mind that's always fully on display;
He always comes out and proves it constantly, multiple times a
day.

Never in my lifetime have I ever seen anyone as bad as this;
I never thought in a million years I'd see if this kind of person
     really exist.
Trump's wreaked havoc big time on the global stage,
And he's put a coffin nail in society, especially during these
     rough times in this day and age.
The big question is, when will his nonsense come to a complete
     halt and stop?
At this point, no one really knows if it will be soon or if it will not.
At this point, we can only cross our toes and cross our fingers;
With a lot of good luck, we hope this B.S. definitely will no
     longer linger.
We've got to have a positive outlook and hope for the best in
     the election in 2024.
Hopefully by then, it'll be the end, and there'll definitely be no
     more.
Like a dog that's always barking, at which time he won't bite;
On the other hand, when Trump stops his barking, we're in for
     an ugly, knock-down, drag-out fight.
I'd like to say something that's never before been mentioned;
Actually, it's my observation that grabbed my focus and attention.
Quite clearly there's shown in all the known evidence,
Trump's never had the mindset or qualities to be president.
In the beginning from the inception of creation,
There's always been an overwhelming expectation
"To at least attempt to love one another, as though they're your
     brothers."

Whenever there's a large number of people Trump has usually led,
Time and again, they follow him blindly, and he's always
        proved to be a knucklehead.
It's widely known nowadays, Trump's facing hell and hard times,
For us patriotic Americans, that's great and really sounds just fine.

TRUMP IS AMERICA'S
#1 FAKE, SLICK, TRICK MASTER!

There's never been any inkling or sign of Trump being elegant
and refined,

He's a knucklehead…YES, so you don't have to guess; it charac-
terizes his personality at best.

It's what sticking out about his personality like a sore thumb,

Revealing he's a crazy person who's dumb.

What was our country thinking, electing him Commander-in-
Chief?

Well…we're going to have to pay for that for years with no relief.

The best and positive lesson from him that was well learned:

He should never be reelected to another term.

We can never, ever make that mistake again in our lives;

That's equal to our whole country committing mass suicide.

It didn't take long to know Trump's I.Q. is not high but really low,

When he started from the beginning, running the country like a
reality show.

He's still always trying to drain and suck money from every-
where he can;

There are a lot of people who're blind of that, because they
really don't want to understand.

Trump's a lifetime negative person who's centered on his selfish
and dumb pride.

Everyone can see that's who he is and what he always tries to
    hide. There's nothing in this world this guy wouldn't do;
He'll even complain about something he didn't like, flip the
    script, and then try to sue.
He's an egotistical maniac, self-centered and non-compassionate
    guy
Who wouldn't care if any statements he's made caused lot of
    people to die.
He doesn't really like people of color and has taken opportuni-
    ties to show his hate.
There are also multiple women out there who've accused him of
    rape.
Watch out America; At all times, always stay on your P's and Q's—
Trump's not finished with his sneaky plots and his nasty, evil
    views.
He's always made asinine statements, and its good he wasn't
    reelected.
He said Vladimir Putin's a genius; from him, that's totally ex-
    pected.
When Trump called him that genius, to Ukraine, that was hor-
    ribly cruel;
To us, it showed he's an idiot and clearly a stupid fool.
Putin's now poopin' on Ukraine, boldly, without any shame;
That move made Trump happy, which proved again he's insane.
Since the invasion started, Trump felt good and still feels fine;
That's how a real knucklehead feels and proves he's the slimiest
    of all time.

It's always been true about crazy people; they always say crazy
things.

That sums up Trump when he opens his mouth; his statements
no longer have any stings.

TRUMP: AMERICA'S TOP DEVIL MINDED AND TRASHY EX-PRESIDENT!

Lately in the news, Trump said, "Putin is a savvy genius."

That comment only proves Trump's really a full-blown fool,

And that's not coming from any comment from any old school.

Keeping his mouth shut is what he'll never do,

Followed by his B.S. always…and with Trump, that's nothing new.

Everyone should keep in mind, and really be rest assured,

When Trump talks, nobody should listen, and he should be
completely ignored.

Everything he talks about are big lies that're definitely absurd,

With enormously big hype, lies, and craziness that's always for
the birds.

The big question is:

What the hell is going on? Where's his brain at?

And what can be on his mind?

Maybe more of his evil, stupid crap.

No one really knows, but it sure shows those signs.

Even he doesn't have a clue, having a brain that's empty all the
time,

It's so tiresome, hearing the same crap from him, constantly and
on a consistent basis.

Most of the things he talks about proves he's a pure bigot and a
straight-up racist.

Trump's on the side of most evil groups—white supremacists
   and neo-Nazi organizations.
When they march and protest in large numbers, he promotes
   their ugly M.A.G.A. demonstrations.
Trump grew up with wealthy parents who were coldblooded to
   him when he was raised;
That's the reason why he doesn't have an inkling about compas-
   sion for those descendants of slaves.
There's an old statement that comes to mind and has been
   around for quite a longtime;
It really fits perfectly, especially now in these days and times.
Trump has a huge hold on a great number of those idiots in his fold.
They're highly educated but really stupid fools;
Having been highly educated at their high-level schools,
Shame on every single one of them
For the negative messages they consistently send.
They won't say or tell anything close to being the truth,
Creating very bad influences all the time on our very fragile
   youth.
They have no real plausible excuse or reason why they're men-
   tally poisoning the youth.
Trump needs to stop his madness right away—not tomorrow,
   but right now.
And he better not try to lie and try to say he doesn't really
   know how!
His messaging is definitely way worse on a higher level than just
   bad,

Adding on to his total genera of being super horrible and super
  sad.
And all good people will feel positive, and they'll be happily
  glad,
When they can say he's done and gone…good riddance to an
  evil and nasty cad!

TRUMP: HIS UGLY, EVIL TRUTH IS REVEALED!

This man has always fanned the flames of hate,

And no doubt in doing so, he's been overwhelmingly great.

The Devil in the flesh, he's proven to have always been;

Deep in the troubling waters of kinds of ugly sin.

Most people can see that's way down deep within his soul;

It's always been there, his most precious and ultimate goal.

Trump still fantasizes about how great (he thinks) he was at the
top;

However, in reality, everyone else everywhere knows he defi-
nitely was not.

If he keeps it up, he'll drive himself into a psychotic mental state,

Much worse than Nixon did when he was involved in Watergate.

The problem is, he keeps lying about the election, saying he won.

He's likely to take that lie to his grave; that's the only way it'll
be completely done.

Also his supporters and cronies keep saying the same lie, too;

They won't let it go either and continue stirring up trouble
starting more bad things new.

It's often said, "You can't teach an old dog new tricks";

That's really true about Trump. He's someone who can't be
changed or fixed;

It's obvious he's definitely set in his foul, evil ways,

And for the rest of eternity, that's how he'll forever stay.

New technologies often help some people get better and change;

Nothing will ever help Donald Trump—he's destined to always
stay the same,

When he was in office, he became history's awful and slimy
most menace,

Proving his mentality is no higher than his former TV show *The
Apprentice*.

When he was in office, he always worked on ways to disrupt
and destroy

Many governmental policies, the same as a hateful little boy.

Trump thinks of Putin as a worldly master and humanity's su-
perior treat;

Everyone else sees them both as coldblooded disasters full of
evil and deceit.

Trump cries "fake news!" lying and saying he's the one who's
always right,

And everything his buddy Putin does is go around the world
picking all kinds of major fights.

Trump and Putin are on the same level and consistently blend,

Continuing on their evil paths of negative, nasty trends.

When Trump's ever been accused of anything, he'll never admit
he did it;

Even when proven wrong, he never comes clean, apologizes,
and will finally admit it.

TRUMP: MASTER OF EVIL AND DARKNESS!

In the media, it was recently reported and revealed,

Trump was really the main one in reverse, perpetrating the
  steal.

In the 2020 election, that was the focus and slimy, ugly deal;,

It really opened up a microscopic look,

To see how much Trump is such a big-time crook.

Nastiness, lies, hate, and racism are just some of the evidences
  on Trump being that crook;

It's all documented and logged unchangeable in the legal books.

It's really difficult to say anything more—

Trump's sliminess is definitely seen and known for sure.

There's nothing good can be said about him, for that matter;

The more that's said grows even sadder and sadder,

Lately, all the destruction and death Russia has caused is serious
  and surely not meaningless.

Putin's buddy Trump has the nerve to go around calling that ty-
  rant a genius.

By no means would a genius start wars, create mayhem, chaos,
  and massive death.

That's at the bottom spectrum of humanity; darkness and evil
  are the only things left.

It's all in Trump's corner, because that's what he'd probably do;

That type of mentality for him is really nothing new.

His sense of morality and rightfulness is not Trump and com-
    pletely done;
His aim is making sure the country never comes together and be
    one.
Any Republican who doesn't bow down to him, he'll go after
    their head,
And whoever chooses not to do so knows in Trump's world,
    they'll be completely dead.
Right now, for Republicans, Trump's the best thing this side of
    the moon,
But when the justice department starts to intensely go after him,
    that's the only place he'll be immune.

TRUMP'S NEVER HAD POSITIVE MENTALITY!

When Trump was in office, he brainwashed millions of Americans;

That's something he focused on and really perfected.

When his mission had been accomplished, it was never rejected;

What he'd done wasn't discovered during that period in time.

Officials must now work constantly and hard to undo all his
crimes,

Working as fast as possible, so America can quickly heal

And make sure no one else can come along and again try to or-
ganize the same attempt to steal.

Republicans have a concern they're trying to but can't ignore;

Their party is splintered and broken like never before.

Major reconstruction is needed, starting at the bottom floor,

Stupid and dumb troubles are tied to Trump as his main thing;

That's what he has facing him and all the trouble it brings.

Always and forever ugliness and nastiness, nothing ever nice.

Eventually, it's going to catch up to him, and he'll definitely pay
the price.

Dumb, stupid, and ugly messes are exactly what you'll get.

Any person who sticks with Trump, you'll be making a bad bet.

Since 2016, the start of him being politically sound,

He's turned this country's system topsy-turvy and upside down.

However, we're moving towards building the country back,

To getting things right again and back on track;

That's the reality of an ever-present fact.

Next question: who or of what next is Trump planning to sue?

Is it someone or something we know about, or is it something
or someone new?

Knowing his crazy mentality, I'll bet he really doesn't have a
clue;

He'll instantly make up his mind and then feverishly try and
pursue.

With that kind of mind set, he'll never do or get anything right;

The only thing he'll be doing is causing another stupid meaning-
less fight.

The good thing is, the D.O.J. has signaled about their accurate
investigations and perceptions;

They're pursuing Trump's records and history with no flaws
and no deceptions.

No one knows what the future might hold;

Staying away from Trump should be our main and ultimate goal.

Never in our country's history has America experienced so
many top-level, illegally vicious crimes;

Donald Trump is responsible for the majority of them, and he's
the worst of all times.

What evil guts and gall this guy definitely has seriously got;

To add on his coldblooded, hateful attitude definitely reveals a
lot.

TRUMP: AMERICA'S MODERN MONSTER!

Early in the beginning of Trump's election campaign,

Evidence proved there wouldn't be anything positive the country would gain;

Bad mouthing Mexicans, Muslims, and others right from the start,

Demonstrated pure evilness, hatefulness, and more with a cold-blooded heart.

Nothing's changed since then; still the same and even worst.

Whenever you think of him, his bad and nasty demeanor comes up first,

And as the old saying goes, "A leopard never changes its spots."

Donald Trump is exactly that way, and no one can say he's not.

Everyone should realize, he'll throw you under the bus,

Because of his long history, to know this and do not to trust.

Wealth, good education, and celebrity status does not make a man;

Having compassion, doing right or wrong when necessary at the right time is a major part of that plan.

He has no real friends; just puppet-people mostly around him.

If Trump didn't have major attention status, they'd quickly down him.

He's disgraced America's image during a meeting while on the world stage;

Trump knows and should've done better, especially a person of
  his age.
European countries and leaders dislike him deeply to their core;
They're greatly relieved he's out of the picture and not Amer-
  ica's leader anymore.
If being a knucklehead was a major college course,
Trump would have a doctorate's degree and be a sought-after
  source,
Or if being a knucklehead was a major federal crime, he'd be
  locked up in prison, doing decades of time.
H.B.C.U.'s have a saying: "The mind is a terrible thing to waste,"
But looking at Donald Trump's case, he's got nothing but
  wasted space.

TRUMP: AMERICA'S UNKEPT WORST SECRET!

It would be our country's worst nightmare if Trump won again
for the top spot,
But if his criminal investigation is successful, his running aspira-
tions will be completely shot.
Trump's motivation toward racial discrimination has his great
admiration with focused preparation, and total dedication.
Due to that conclusion, the only positive solution to those af-
fected: Get complete retribution.
We're hoping there'd be no pain and suffering caused by any
domestic terroristic cults;
If that happened to be the result, Donald Trump would be defi-
nitely at fault.
If anyone living today died because of Trump tomorrow,
He definitely wouldn't act or show any signs of remorse or sorrow.
When there's nothing lost, there's nothing gained; Trump will
always Trump and stay the same,
And he will never ever change, to prove he's definitely insane.
Just pause for a moment and take a deep breath;
Wrap your mind around Trump's actions, then you'll be pre-
pared for what to expect.
We've got to have hope for this to be the end and complete
scope,
Because all of Donald Trump's crappy B.S. is not at all any joke.

It's not hard connecting the dots to all his coldblooded spots;

I'm hoping it'll confirm, change, and/or completely stop

His evil ugly plan of running another negative plot.

I hope you've taken into account what Trump's put the country
through;

Nothing ever changes, and nothing's ever new.

There's an old saying that says, "The more things change, the
more they stay the same,"

So, with Mr. Trump mixed in that quote, that's the fame to his
game.

TRUMP: A BURNED OUT AFTER THOUGHT!

Trump's really pissed off, not being born heir to a throne;

Thank GOD that didn't happen! He'd be in the stratosphere in
places unknown.

With righteousness, goodness, mercy, and compassion void of
Trump's morality and thought,

Narrow minded thinking is all he was raised up with and taught.

He's always shown to have limited capacity in his brain;

When a person can't fathom that much, there's little he can gain.

It's a pity the people around him are being led by their noses

Wherever he wants to take them and whatever new lies he pro-
poses—

Those kinds of people, so-to speak, are pressed deeply under his
thumb;

That shows a lack of intelligence really some would call stupid
and dumb.

A healthy mentality is about being a person open-minded and free;

Being hoodwinked and bamboozled by Trump is not where I'd
want to be.

Focusing on Republicans, eat knucklehead sandwiches, served
daily, and on a plate,

That's what Trump has always fed them; that's what they al-
ways ate.

Trump's got 'em, hook line and sinker, and they'll never get away;

You can bet your bottom dollar, they'll always be there to stay.

Tomorrow's always a new day, so what's on Trump's feeble
mind?

I'm sure he's probably cooking up something good, and we'll
know very soon in due time.

I've got to give it to Trump; he is the master of deception,

Which means we've got to be on our toes and sense his initial
perceptions.

When we were kids growing up, we used to play hide and go
seek;

I'll bet Donald Trump was good at that game and probably was
a super freak.

TRUMP WITH HIS SMALL BRAIN, SUFFERS FROM GREAT MENTAL DISABILITIES!

Hey America, it's way past time to raise the red flag;

Trump's starting again to boast and brag,

And the next step you know what he's gonna do:

Make up some fake reason about why and who he's going to sue.

We all know that's what Trump does; we've got his actions
down pat.

You can read him like an open book; the facts are the facts.

He thinks running to Mar-a-Lago can help him continue his
ugly, stupid schemes and things,

But the feds are gonna go there with all kinds of implicating
legal stings.

Ready or not, Donald. Here they come!

You better have things in order; for you, it's not going to be fun.

Mark my words, you'll be under a microscope, especially nowa-
days;

You'll be thoroughly scrutinized and, at that point, can't be
saved.

When putting the pressure on Trump, he usually gets real mad;

He'll then get desperate, react, and then do something bad.

You don't need a playbook to counter his actions;

We've experienced all his scenarios and what next will happen.

Then he'll say something off the record and behind the scenes;

It'll be something truthful but nasty and ugly…you know what
    I mean.
He's the kind of person who'll do something as fast as you can
    blink,
Then comes up with some excuse faster than you can think,
    "That really stinks."
Trump has a completely twisted and evil mind;
That's the main reason for the country's present twisted living
    conditions and bad times.
There's an old saying, "Sticks and stones may break my bones…"
However, we must stay on track and stick with the facts,
And keep up the trend to finalize Trump's political end.
Never play games and stop his political gain and halt his ques-
    tionable fame.
Throw his a— under the bus and turn his dark image into dust!
Trump and his twisted ideologies are always ongoing problems;
It's going to take many collaborating minds to come together
    and solve them.
His brain for life is dumb, numb, and drained,
Completely and definitely retracted from any positive mental
    gains.
Trump's like a wino, addicted and hooked on wine
Who suffers from poor health and absolute great mental decline.

TRUMP: REPUBLICANS' TOP PARTY POOPER!

There's a kids' rhyme Trump could appropriately use in these
days and times:
"Apples, peaches, and pumpkin pie,"
If you want to make America great again, I'm your guy;
However, we all know, that's a bunch of dirty crap, and what
will he really do
Is put the country in more deep s—t and more of a nasty stew.
From my viewpoint, and what we all have seen and presently
agree,
He's now putting something together that'll be really crazy.
Trump's a real underhanded sleazeball and makes us always guess;
Whatever the new thing he's doing, usually turns out to be an
unadulterated mess.
Losing his reelection bid turned out to be a great blessing for us;
We won't have to experience a president who's childish, shows
anger, evilness, and distrust.
This can be characterized as great positivity, moving in the right
direction and more;
Thank GOD we don't have to deal with a person we would
rather basically ignore.
There's loads of information in the public records about Trump
on the legal books,

Proving the fact of him being a low life conman, and a dirty crook.

If he was an average citizen, he'd have a long-listed criminal file

For everyone to see his long life, history, and dark lifestyle.

He's always been saying his life is private, and that's personal
information;

However, the system doesn't work like that when you're the
leader of our nation.

What's really devastating and a hard cold main fact,

After all he's done, and what continues to happen, he's still try-
ing by any means to get back!

Americans are not dumb; we're just numb from all the damage
he's done, and it's not been fun.

We all remember and know Trump was impeached not once,
but twice;

That's proof of a bad and evil person definitely out of the ques-
tion of being nice.

There are Trump allies, which should be dumped too;

It's good to see there's not too many who really like him, only
just a few.

In a recent interview, Trump was asked to condemn Putin, and
he chose to decline;

That response sends out a horrible, chilling message, and a real
dark and ugly sign.

Trump's still in control of the Republicans after all he's said and
done;

Whether they like him or not, he'll not be easily overtaken and
completely undone.

TRUMP: ALWAYS BAD, ON THE DARKSIDE!

The important issue up front is: It's time for Trump to be
  dumped!
Overall, it's always one thing after another…oh brother!
What comes next is, what more negativity will we discover?
He's always doing a lot behind closed doors and under the
  table;
Very sneaky, a cheat, and slimy, his name fits with those being
  appropriate labels.
Mind- and vision-less, he thinks money and power is everything;
Any person who doesn't have GOD's righteousness, wisdom,
  and knowledge, they'll never have anything.
Trump's shiftless, arrogant, hateful, and lazy;
All those attributes make the man super ignorant and crazy.
That's the only category which he's best at and number one;
The only person who comes close to him is his oldest son.
That sums up his family as we well know and definitely can see;
There's no doubt about it, and we all do whole heartedly agree.
Of course, Trump's going to say, this is all bogus and a big lie;
You know what's coming next from him—he's that kind of guy.
The saying is, if you walk a mile in any man's shoes,
It'll let you know exactly what he'll say or do.
Always keep in mind, the older Trump gets, it's apparent and
  you can bet,

Things will always worsen, because he's clearly not done yet.

Trump feels real good when things always go real bad;

That's called a hateful and evil mentality, and that's really sad.

Trump's a big-time, crooked hustler, and America's his biggest
    ever gig.

We all must realize and understand that, and we must stop him
    and renege.

To all the people out there who are dedicated and on his side:

Trump's using your values against you and using your morality
    and pride,

You better wake up and realize this before his 2024 election run.

If you can't see that's what's happening, it'll be too late, and all
    will be completely done.

He tried to manipulate the postmaster general's job, creating
    voter suppression by mail;

We've got to stay on top of that issue to ensure that scheme ulti-
    mately fails.

Decades from now, it'll be written, void of any mystery—

Donald Trump will be the most horrible and ruthless president
    ever elected in history.

TRUMP: DARK AND EVIL IDEOLOGIST!

Trump's bad and dark narrative always seems to choke.

When he starts ranting and raving about some kind of stupid hoax,

His word you can't just believe and isn't all that strong;

The result from that turns out to be, every time, he's always
wrong.

We're supposed to have the best person for the presidency
elected,

Not the top guy getting into office who's financially and politi-
cally connected.

The president's job is focusing on the country's safety and secu-
rity, number one,

Not thinking his job is like a game show, and it's all just hap
hazard, lollygagging, and fun,

Everyone someday, somehow, will eventually have to pay their dues;

It's on each one of us seriously to decide exactly which road we
will choose.

We've always been taught there's a thin line between love and
hate;

Everyone has to make up their minds to dwell badly or make
life great.

Nonchalant mentality isn't good for anyone's soul;

The right thing to do good moving forward is to have positive
goals.

Moving away from Trumpism is the right and a positive start;
It's definitely great for our minds and especially great for our
    hearts.
Human nature has always had to choose between doing right or
    wrong;
Choosing the right direction has always been good and made us
    strong.
The 2024 election is going to be an important key;
We've got to pull together if we're going to live in harmony.
Trump dishonoring our modern society must not continue for
    long;
If we don't make that transition soon, our democracy will even-
    tually be gone.
In 2024, if Trump is able to somehow pull off a win again,
America will be in bad shape and possibly never be able to mend.
And if he loses the election, you know just what he'll do:
Lie and claim he was cheated again, and then see who he can sue.

TRUMPISM IS JUST AS BAD AS PRISON!

We all know how he performed as president with all his games;
If he should get into office again, look out, it'll all be the same.
A major decision Trump made was to undermine the European
and N.A.T.O. alliance;
He made an extra effort to focus on not being at all compliant.
That's not making America in the world's view number one;
Tearing our credibility down where he could is what he had done.
That's what a little brain, small mind will ultimately do,
Never having the ability to deeply think things thoroughly
through.
Never forget, always remember—Trump will be Trump.
That's why we've always said it's past time for him to be dumped.
What more evidence does anyone need?
We've got to rid him of our system with excessive speed.
The opposition for him is very high and tight;
We know we're in for a hard and possibly bitter dogfight.
Our humanity has to take over and absolutely be the best judge,
Not from any position of holding any kind of long-term grudge.
We know from past history, that's not what Trump would do;
He holds deep, angry grudges against people all the time and
makes sure to see them through.
A leader of the free world is supposed to be calm and be about
peace;

That's not how Trump operates—not at all in the least!

Our democracy is coming back from being on the line;

If Trump has anything to do or say about it, it'll continue to decline.

He really has not cared for that issue, whatever which way,

Just as long as it doesn't affect his rich luxurious lifestyle, mak-
ing sure it's never fazed.

When Trump had a chance to help Ukraine, his answer was a
flat out no;

Now the President Biden's helping Ukraine, the Republicans
said he's moving much to slow.

TRUMP:
HIS EVIL, HATEFULNESS KEEPS GOING!

When Donald Trump was president, he was like a drunk driver,
    steering in the wrong direction,
Or like a severe sickness or disease, creating a greater infection.
This modern world is moving and changing fast every day,
Forever trying to move forward peacefully in a positive way.
Trump's never in any way been a part of any positive actions;
The only thing he's been focused on is negative, hateful distractions.
When a person in the free world has the gall to say Putin's a genius,
It really proves he's a real nut job, and his outrageous words are
    serious but meaningless.
When Trump had the nerve to make such an awfully stupid claim,
Again it proves he's got a screw loose and an insane brain.
Only people on the other side will take Trump at his word;
There's also those who'll still stick with him even though they
    know he's absurd.
Trump and Putin are two peas in a pod, and both are big-time thugs.
Mark my word, that's the truth and can't be swept under the rug.
Trump's not finished; there's a lot more he's going to say,
So let's make sure he fails 2024 on Election Day.
Cheating and scheming are his focus and stellar expertise;
When the 2024 election comes around, he'll ramp it up and
    won't decrease,

And IF he wins, it'll be devastating for everyone in our nation,

Quite possibly have a ripple effect for future generations.

Critically important strategies must be worked on and done,

Making sure Trump can't say he was cheated again, and he
really won.

Trump IS the bull in a China shop,

Destroying everything he touches, disrupting everything, and
never stops.

All the things Donald Trump over the years has been known to do

Is the same old thing as usual, and to no surprise; nothing new.

Whatever ugly statement Trump makes

Can be proven to have been falsely prefabricated, at any rate,

And be incorrect on updates.

He lies, saying he's making America great, while facing multiple
legal negative cases on upcoming dates.

TRUMP'S EXCEEDINGLY
THE MOST RUTHLESS EVER!

Donald Trump is history's number one trick master,

And it boils down to say he's our greatest disaster.

He's really strange; he's like a runaway train looking for politi-
cal gain.

Again, I must say, there'll come a time, when he'll pay for his
political crimes—

To be specific, it's called the big pay back; it's on track and a
real fact.

Putin's now certified a war criminal, and that's by his design;

Donald Trump idolizes him, and that proves he has an evil, in-
sane mind.

Hypothetically, if nonintelligence was a crime, Trump would
end up doing major prison time.

Since Trump's been in politics, life in America has been very
uneasy;

It's sad to say it's that way because Trump is very sleazy.

When he announced his candidacy, and he started his campaign
and ran,

That's when his slimy evilness and bigot actions showed up and
began.

Trump's degraded the presidency to a lower level, which never
happened before;

All Americans must keep that in mind when voting and never
let it be ignored.

All living former presidents are against him and his actions, and
they disagree;

They all know he's not qualified for the job—definitely that's
what they see.

Seeking GOD's blessings, Trump doesn't go in that direction,
and his focus is wrong,

Because he's a hateful, evil, nasty bigot; those are the areas
where he's very strong.

We shouldn't really be surprised when Trump revealed, he's on
Putin's side.

When he made that statement, he didn't hide and said it with
pride.

Putin spreads many lies, almost as much as Trump;

That's the most important reason why they both must be com-
pletely dumped.

Trump has a few people of color bamboozled, because they
really like his theme.

It seems as though they've forgotten Dr. King's speech; he had a
bigger and better dream.

We must pay attention to his bigotry documented over many years;

Trump's always proved to be a racist individual, and he's made
that very clear.

TRUMP: TRASHED HOPEFULLY AND DUMPED!

Trump's theme of white supremacy will eventually have to take
a knee,

Because every American in our country is equally free.

That's one thing the majority of citizens completely do agree:

The M.A.G.A. crowds and hate groups, their knees will also
eventually bend,

And all the violence and chaos, thankfully, will come com-
pletely to an end.

We said in 2016, when he came in, "Hello Trump, and goodbye
sanity,"

Because what he started was on the line; especially our humanity.

"Never say never," that's what went on; we all expected and felt

During his term in office that was his attitude, and that's what
he coldbloodedly dealt.

The reality of everything he was doing was shocking and very
painful;

It should have been totally the opposite, more meaningful, posi-
tive, and gainful,

But that's the result of dealing with someone who has a closed
and narrow mind.

It's always proven to be a fact—it happens all the time.

Roses are red and violets are blue;

Let's make Trump past history and pray it definitely comes true!

When Trump became president, he thought he was made our
country's KING.

American democracy is not structured that way; that's our con-
stitutional main thing.

All our citizens are free and equal; he doesn't realize and understand.

That's a part of our core values and basic to our brand,

May I end by saying that is ultimately the overall big picture?

Everyone, even Trump, must realize that; if so, it'll make us
mentally richer.

TRUMP'S EVIL BIGOTRY MUST BE STOPPED AT ALL COST!

Trump's buddy Putin is being called a dictator of an evil empire;

That's the exact same dream of Donald J. Trump's ultimate desire.

All his statements and actions have shown to be quite similar to that,

And if he should get back into office again, he'll demonstrate
   it's really a true fact.

He's proven to always dislike the ways of our country's democracy;

On the other hand, he seems to favor a structured autocracy.

Our country can't and won't stand for those types of feelings
   and actions,

And America definitely doesn't need any more of his crazy dis-
   tractions.

Most of Trump's decisions are really way out of bounds.

In fact, the majority of his talking points are logically unsound
   and profound.

And he's always done things that don't stand on any solid ground.

Stopping Trump from moving back into the White House, I
   think will be a major but achievable task;

We're calling on all good citizens to come out and vote him
   down, so please, that's all we ask.

Liking and cheering for Putin is crazy and definitely not right.

That evidence shows; let's make sure Trump doesn't get another
   chance, and it's clearly within our sight.

It's also obvious he's not mentally the kind of leader our coun-
try is structured for;
It's very plain and it's simply out in the open—something we
cannot and should not ignore.
It was horrible we had to suffer for four years with him being
the boss at the top;
That's why at all cost, this time, he's got to be shut down and
completely stopped.
Everything Trump arrogantly stands for has always been ugly
and totally incorrect;
Every citizen in this country must be shown and treated with
the utmost compassion and gracious undying respect.
Trump's never in his life's been a GODfearing man;
That's something he deeply has never been and truly doesn't un-
derstand.
His mental sanity is doubtful and in serious question
When he ignorantly said the war in Ukraine was the result of
the 2020 rigged election.
That statement proves he probably has a seriously diseased
brain that's suffering an infection.
How can any sane person seriously equate the two?
It's all up to GOD and not between me and you.

TRUMP: A FAILURE ALWAYS LOOKING FOR MANY WAYS TO FAIL!

All of Trump's life, he's been liar and creep;

The exact same thing as president: He was command liar and
creep,

And he's definitely now known as a dirty sneak and a sex freak.

All those negatives toward him are his only and are very unique.

Lately, he asked Putin to find lies about Joe Biden's son;

This shows he's still doing things that are very evil, stupid, and
dumb.

We could go on for years, proving Trump's dark and ugly crap.

That's his focus and only nature; that's the only way he'll ever act.

All Trump supporters always just narrowly think

It's like leading a horse to water and trying to make him drink.

The more you try and tell them, the more they defy and get strong;

They'll never admit to being on the right side of being the ones
who are wrong.

All the hate groups and Trump supporters like him are really
premature;

They better find out why he's for them and how long they'll
have to endure.

If they know what's good for them, they better be sure.

Hey, hey, what's there to say?

Knuckleheads are out there, each and every day.

It comes a time you ask yourself, what can you really do?

The only thing is just bite the bullet; it's all really the same and
    really nothing new.

It's shocking all the important people and officials on Trump's side

Must make a decision, because if I were in their shoes, it's time
    to find some place to hide.

I guess they're thinking is, "At this juncture, what else is there
    to lose?"

That old proverbial kitchen sink, and anything else they use;

Trump's on a tear to nowhere, because he really don't care,

And it all amounts to putting them in a place of total despair.

When a decent person looks around,

They hope they can say they've finally found

The pursuit of moving towards the good life,

So all you can do is stand up and fight

And continue to pursue everything that's right.

TRUMP: HIS NEGATIVE STORY HASN'T STOPPED!

Trump is responsible for old-fashioned, medieval crimes;

He's still doing the same in these modern times.

History shows he's executed mostly cynical, negatively pinnacle
    decisions,

Proving he has not an inkling of any positive visions.

I'm at my wits end about all those at Trump's defense—a per-
    son of this kind

Who clearly shown he's not right and out of his mind.

It's devastating to find the evilness and hate he likes to propagate;

He does it all astoundingly, and he doesn't hesitate.

The courts shut down all his coldblooded hopes

To stop people of color the right to vote,

And the majority of Republicans were in on it, too,

All the ones who tried to help were more than just a few.

As you can see, the blame and shame game has not changed and
    is still the same;

It's always very strong and continues to live on without any let
    up in sight.

Knowing that's what it is, we must continue our hard and ag-
    gressive fight.

Life can change quickly in a feasible amount of time;

Surely logically, we all know that's not a crime;

That's human nature, definitely without a doubt.

It's all within humanity—we just have to bring it out.

How does Trump profess he's doing right when we know he's
doing wrong?

He's the kind of person who won't admit it, even after he's
gone.

We can only stick out this problem and wait until he's com-
pleted his trend;

Work as hard as we can to bring him down completely at the end.

We'll do what we have to, I guess, to stop all his ugly mess.

Bottom line: This will all lead to another massive test.

Keep in mind, we've got to keep up this enormous fight

In the name of humanity, focused on doing what's right.

All of America has got to stand up and say, "That's it—stop—
no more!" and "It's enough!"

We're no longer going to put up with his evil, hateful stuff.

There's been hundreds of times describing Trump's illegal, evil,
and nasty ways…

We used up almost everything in the book; there's nothing more
that much to say!

EVIL, NASTY, AND UGLINESS
IS TRUMP'S REGULAR THEME!

Lately, with documented atrocities of war crimes, death, and
tyranny committed by Putin;
Trump still calls him a man who's very smart.
That statement definitely proves he's non-compassionate and
very coldblooded basically at heart.
The world situation nowadays is highly and extremely dire;
Knowing all that, Trump should never again be the one we
want to rehire.
And surely he's not the one who can lead us out of this quagmire.
His hateful, nasty ego is very horrible for sure:
It's shameful his supporters can't see that; they love him and
he's highly adored.
Moving forward, it seems we're under some type of Trumpism
curse…
What he does and says, things always tend to end up getting worse.
What did America ever do to deserve negativity and evil like this?
Could be our up and down history…there are many things on
that list.
Because of all the 2022 current horrible events,
Everyone can see clearly Donald Trump's negative intent.
It's been two years, and he keeps lying, saying the election was a
great big steal,

Even though all pertinent, truthful, and honest evidence has already been revealed.

He tries to say his lies are correct, and that he's really number one,

And that really covers Trump's overall focus—that's the only real thing he's ever done.

Arithmetic adds up all the time—one plus one equals two.

That's also exactly Donald Trump's bottom line. There's really nothing new.

He also thinks the average citizen can't comprehend all his lies and dirty, sneaky actions.

That's why he continues to create all the time a thousand and one distractions.

There are those in his inner circle with possible prosecutions being considered;

It's surprising how they can say many foul things and showing they're awfully bitter.

Tell me, what kind of message does all that probably send?

It's not over; there'll comes a time they'll do it all over again.

For whatever B.S. is in him usually will come up first;

Donald always turns up thinking that's his real worth.

All his people who go down in scandal, he considers them just routine collateral damage;

And whatever their outcome turns out to be—no problem; he feels he'll be able to manage.

Always being devilish and promoting a bunch of dirty, nasty lies,

Trump does that all the time routinely and will never, ever try to hide.

THE TRUMP TREND MUST COME TO AN END!

It's absolutely ridiculous how Trump lies about old fashion humane normality;

His thoughts and actions on that seriousness are deeply seated in ugly abnormalities.

And how he thinks, he's on the brink of really in need of a shrink.

Please keep in mind how history will see Trump's legacy and how it's defined:

He'll be seen as coldblooded and dark with an ugly, negative mind.

The good nature that's in most people, you can see easily all the time;

When it comes to Trump, there's definitely no inkling and completely no sign,

And that has all been building up over a great period of time.

It's finally known, and the evidence has shown, Trump is officially a criminal,

And all the charges have been determined to be serious and not minimal,

It's never been complicated for anyone in life to treat people nice—

Definitely not in any category or costing any price.

In our society, Trump's attitude and negativity definitely isn't sustainable;

We're moving toward a more positive America, quite necessary
and more attainable.

We must always go to the highest heights, always doing what's
humanly right
For every human being in the country and within sight.
By doing that, there won't be a dispute or kind of fight.
What's needed now is a total plan of a systemic solution
To stopping Trump and Trumpism's ugly, negative societal pollution.
One solution to start working is to combat
All his B.S. and his negative crap.
Thank GOD the country's moving towards normalization, just
as we had before,
Hopefully moving away from four years of Trump and never
taking his mess anymore.
It's a Herculean task to make right the things Trump made
wrong;
We must stay together and toe the mark and always stay mo-
rally strong.
The world of Trump and Trumpism has got to come completely
to a close;
Truth and doing right for all people must be wholeheartedly
proposed.
This is a new day and a new way to promote positivity for all in
the coming years,
Not leaving behind for future generations negative, dark, and
ugly Trump fears.

Our country's overall mentality of hatred and division against
   one another
Has got to come to a stop, and at least just respecting each
   other.

TRUMP: A DYING LEGACY IS COMING TO AN END!

Trump and Putin together; that's what'll be documented in history:

Both extremely big liars and no doubt not even any mystery.

And how much Trump passionately admires him is the bottom line;

It's been thoroughly documented throughout a great period of time.

How the saying goes: "Birds of a feather always flock together."

Trump has always wanted to see Putin and Russia at the international very top;

That's his main focus and where his mind is completely on lock.

When it comes to Putin, Trump has not a bad thing to say; nothing never at all.

And all Putin is wanting to see is a complete annihilation of Ukrainians so they'll completely fall.

Politicians who are being endorsed by Trump really don't care;

They know they'd better go along with him and not against him or feel his angry despair.

Trump rules over those people with a heavy, iron fist,

And they better not stand up and speak out, even think about trying to resist.

More evidence on what Trump has done is increasing in huge amounts;

It's getting to be so much evidence, it's really hard to keep up
the count!

So many things have come up; no one can imagine what the
ending might be.
This time, Trump won't be able to say, "Oh it's other people,
and definitely not me!"
Good riddance to bad rubbish, that what I've always said!
Making sure all the riff raff is cleaned out and gone—in other
words, politically dead.

A KNOCK-KNOCK STATEMENT FOR DONALD TRUMP'S SUPPORTERS AND FRIENDS, ESPECIALLY DURING HIS TERM UNTIL THE END

Knock, knock!

"Who's there?"

"Donald Trump. If you don't like me, I really don't care!"